YOUR TRUE COLOURS

Intentions and Reflections to Deepen Self-Awareness

Sinead Moylett

FriesenPress

One Printers Way
Altona, MB R0G 0B0
Canada

www.friesenpress.com

Copyright © 2024 by Sinead Moylett
First Edition — 2024

Illustrator: Sarah Moylett

All rights reserved.

ISBN
978-1-03831-407-9 (Hardcover)
978-1-03831-406-2 (Paperback)
978-1-03831-408-6 (eBook)

SELF-HELP, AFFIRMATIONS

Distributed to the trade by The Ingram Book Company

For my daughter, Sarah. You have inspired my healing journey just by your existence. Singing "True Colours" to you the night you were born was intuitive and fitting. Singing it to you as I'd tuck you into sleep many nights, many years following was an honour I'll never take for granted.

Being your mother is the greatest gift I have
ever received.
I see your True Colours, sweet pea, and that's why I
love you . . . with absolute ease.
You are enough.
You are so worthy of peace, love, and happiness.
Thank you for choosing me as your Mama.

& for Mum (my angel above) and for Dad. I love you so dearly.

Table of Contents

Foreword

I have gotten to the other side of a lot of challenges, of wounding, of being unseen and unheard. I have lived through very confusing situations and situations that compromised my sense of worth in the world. I have done a lot of work, starting in the name of my daughter, and then more anchored in self-love, to heal. I have done years of legwork. I have collected and absorbed messages from healers, light workers, yoga teachers, podcasters, and inspiration from the voice of my higher self—when I finally began to connect with her. I have studied and poured into myself, words and language and intentions and reflections that have changed me and healed me. I am here to offer these to you, in this book of intentions and reflections. An offering of what I have learned. We are in times of change, dismantling, and deep healing. If you're reading this, it's because you are leaning into your own personal journey of healing and growth. I hope the words in these pages inspire you to reflect on what's possible for the greatest expression of your life.

Introduction

I have lovingly curated this book over three and a half years, writing and sharing the lessons I have learned in my own healing and self-discovery journey. I have offered every one of these intentions and reflections in my role as a yoga teacher.

The deepest discovery of our True Colours—our truest, most authentic self, underneath the challenging experiences of life—happens when we look within and heal all the parts that need and deserve healing. In these pages, I share my heart with you. The intentions and reflections in this book have brought me to the place I am today, a place where my relationship to myself is the most loving and compassionate it has ever been.

There are two hundred and forty-two offerings in this book, rather than three hundred and sixty-five. As I approached two hundred and forty-two, the book felt complete; forcing the rest didn't feel right or authentic. I remembered that two hundred and forty-two is an angel number that I have aligned with in the past. It means "Stability and Harmony Await You." When you see this number, your guardian angels are signaling that balance and stability—found in realizing your True Colours—are coming your way. With the reflection opportunities in these pages, I believe you can, and will, get to know yourself and your True Colours on a new, balanced and stable level.

It is also a reminder to us that integration is key to healing, growth, self discovery, and a stronger sense of self-awareness. Taking the journey to your True Colours requires "days off," to allow your journey to settle in your heart. Use these days to take a break from inner work, simply living and enjoying the benefits of this journey. Rest matters, and so do you.

There are five healing reflections throughout the book. I am a certified (conscious, connected, circular) Breathwork Facilitator. Within this deep healing practice, after the active breath, I read a reflection to the group as they continue to move through and release emotion. I'd like to share some of those reflections with you, in hopes that they will bring you comfort and healing along your journey.

Discover your true colours through this journey, and become the most beautiful expression of *your* humanity, in this life.

How To Use This Book: Self-Discovery *Does* Take Mindful Effort

You have options; you can use a blend of all four practices, or you can create your own practice, catered to your needs.

Daily Practice

Begin each day reading an intention. Let it sit with you and be with you as you move through your day. End the day by reading the reflection. Process by reading the true colours sentiment and meditating or journaling about your experience, your thoughts, your feelings.

Yoga Practice

Teachers, yoga students, meditation seekers: use this book to set a heart-centred intention for your practices. Close your practice in reading the reflection. You may consider offering discussion groups, using the True Colours offering, following your class.

Intuition Calls

Where intuition calls, simply flip the book open and see where you've been guided.

Table of contents

By reviewing the table of contents, you may see a title that captures your attention. There are also topics that pertain to specific times of the year and the table of contents will help guide you there.

New Year 1

Intention
Be gentle with yourself as a new year begins. Create new patterns, refusing to return to the lie that we are only working hard if we are busy, stressed, and overwhelmed. This can take us out of the rested state cultivated during the holidays faster than we'd like. Choose a different energy. A thoughtful, mindful pace that protects your peace.

Sometimes, taming the mind can be like taming a wild horse. Realizing this is a step toward progress, as you are becoming the witness of your thoughts rather than attaching to them and letting them run you like that wild horse.

Today, invite the remembering that you can be in a state of peace and ease and still be working hard.

Reflection
Be gentle with yourself. Hold onto the rested, peaceful mind. Your peace is productive. Your peace matters, as do you. Be gentle with yourself with daily intention.

True Colours
How were you gentle with yourself today? How can you be gentle with yourself tomorrow?

New Year 2

Intention
Are you taking with you everything you loved about the holidays? Are you letting go and leaving behind everything you didn't?

In our yoga practice, we strengthen our power in all ways. We do this in life, too. Our power to show up, our power to take good energy with us, energy that lights us up and fuels us, that inspires us and motivates us. Our power to leave everything that doesn't light us up behind, like voices of the inner critic, stress, worry. We do this, whether it's through yoga or walking or dancing, because we need an outlet. We all need an outlet that empowers us, heals us, strengthens us, and softens us. Let your outlet hold space for you and empower you just as often as you need it this year.

Reflection
Leave everything you don't need behind. The worry, the busy mind, the stress—none of the things that help anything be better. Take with you the calm, the strength, the ease, the focus, and the softening. All the things that help everything be better.

True Colours
What are you taking with you today from your outlet? What are you leaving behind?

New Year 3

Intention
While there is a whole new year ahead, the foundation of our work remains the same. To simply be here, be present for this moment and the next. Let the gifts of each day be full of presence. Being so attuned to now that you realize the big yet simple truth: life is in the moments. One moment at a time, one love-filled decision at a time.

Be brave, be authentic, be inclusive, lean into discomfort, listen to learn, seek to understand. Let the power of presence and the power of love lead it all; every single moment of now.

Reflection
Let presence be the foundation of each moment this year. Do the next right thing, lead with love that is turned both outwards and inwards. Learn, grow, inspire, challenge, rest, restore, replenish, repeat. In all your days this year, be true to you.

True Colours
Write a loving, supportive letter to yourself about the year you'd like to create. Talk about the energy you'll tap into and the dreams you want to realize. Envision then embody as you live and create.

Fall

Intention
The season of letting go. Lessons from nature, from trees, teach us that letting go makes space for rest and new growth. There is so much we allow ourselves to be defined by, whether good or bad and it can be easy to build our identity around everything we experience. The tree that lets its leaves fall every season, trusts that new

leaves will come, they'll be new, they'll be different, and the cycle will repeat. The tree doesn't resist the process of letting go.

Reflection
Where have your experiences created identity and limitations? Good or bad. Perhaps you're an excellent chef, but perhaps that's not all you are. Letting go can be a mindset that gives way to what's possible outside of limitation. Letting go can be a mindset that chooses not to bring forward ideas, feelings, beliefs that stifle us from growth.

True Colours
What has surfaced? What will you choose to let go of to make space for what's possible? To make space for new growth.

A New Month Begins

Intention
It's a new month a month where expansion can become available. Your growth can be gentle now. Let yourself exhale some of the weight you've been carrying to allow the voice of your higher self to be heard. Where they'll surely remind you; you've go this!

Reflection
It's a new month, your growth can be gentle now. Let the events of last month settle in or wash away. You'll know which is necessary.

True Colours
What did last month teach you? What lessons can you bring with you? What experiences can be released?

Compliments

Intention
You are amazing. When you get compliments like this, do you take them in? Accept them as truth? Receive them? Or do you resist them, even deny them?

Consider that when it is difficult to receive a compliment, two things are happening: you are feeding the lie that so many of us carry that we are not enough. You are also denying the person offering the compliment their honest view of you. Compliments are reflections of your true self.

Reflection
Allow for compliments, for the feedback about who you are, the impact you have, and all the beautiful ways you are showing up in the world.

You are worthy and those complementing you; they are speaking truth.

True Colours
What was the last compliment you received? Discuss it, reflect on it, or write about it. Acknowledge it as truth.

Stillness

Intention
In stillness, we receive the most clarity. Sometimes, we even hear messages we are trying to resist and avoid. Claiming that you don't have time for stillness, for pockets of quiet in your day, only depends on what you choose to prioritize.

Reflection
In a society where we often prioritize productivity, let's change the idea of what productivity looks like. Doing nothing is productive. It allows us to reflect, to rest, to recover and heal. Taking the time to just be and to feel is productive.

Practice being still. Sit or lie comfortably in the discomfort of stillness until it feels like home.

True Colours
Be still for three minutes. Perhaps five. How did that feel?

Living with Intentionality

Intention
Bring awareness to your physical body. Allow your whole body to exhale, to soften. We are in the midst of significant transformation. To move through this journey with more ease, we can choose to live with intentionality. Brining clear intention to the way we breathe, the way we move, to our conversations, our decisions, our relationships and the words we choose. Letting intentionality be a tool to support your individual transformation. Letting intentionality be the replacement for any future regrets.

Reflection
Intentionality helps us to nurture a positive mindset and reminds us of our power to influence purpose, joy and peace in our lives.

True Colours
Start a new day with the concept of intention at the forefront. Move through the day with precise intention in all things. What shifted?

Valentine's Day Self Love

Intention
Valentine's Day. Celebrate and nurture the love you have for your-self, for being so special. Reminding yourself, you ARE special. There's no one like you. Your uniqueness makes you special. No one has experienced the exact life you have, the moments, the challenge, the elation. When you love yourself, you release the need for love that doesn't align with your values. When you love yourself you attract love that can only match it.. and you'll know when it doesn't. Turn the huge doses of love you pour out to others, inward in these next few moments. Let it be free flowing and warm. Perhaps even whisper "I love you."

Reflection
On this day that honours love of all kinds, honouring that love is love is love... Allow some of the love you pour out so freely, to turn inward. Be still, as a reminder of how much you matter. That filling your cup matters because you are so special.

True Colours
Write a love letter to yourself. Let your heart dictate the words. The mind can sit this one out xo

Growth Through Discomfort

Intention
Tension and discomfort are necessary for growth and evolution in the world *and* in your life. Can you think of a time where you went through a challenge you didn't grow from? Or growth that wasn't uncomfortable, even painful? So, knowing this, why would we create suffering on top of the discomfort and tension we are

already experiencing? Why? When we know, we have admitted in *this* moment, that there is always growth on the other side of challenge. Instead, consider trusting all your challenges and say "ah, I see, I am growing".

Reflection
Where did you grow today or in your practice? Can you come back to that very first lesson we were presented with in the world? Leaving the womb, the comfort and safety of the womb and going through the painful, traumatic experience of being born. While we don't remember this experience, it was our first lesson, that after challenge comes expansion and growth; Without fail.

During the chaotic and uncertain times we are in, maybe you can find greater ease by trusting that there will be growth on the other side of it all. & Know that your trusting and peaceful energy will ripple into the world around you.

True Colours
What is causing you discomfort right now? Can you look at the discomfort and ask what is it trying to teach you?

People-Pleasing

Intention
How did we become people pleasers? Pleasing others, looking to create *their* joy, and compromising your own. Looking, ultimately, for their validation of you. Their validation that you are a good person.

Consider that this is a question that comes out of trauma. If I think I am not enough, because of what happened to me or because I had to deal with what happened to me alone, then I look for more validation from the world around me. The truth is, you already are enough. This truth exists, even without external validation.

Reflection
Your biggest contribution to humanity is your own self-realization, your healing and enlightenment. Loving yourself like you needed to be loved, validating yourself like you validate others, so freely. Turn your gaze inward and love yourself unconditionally and authentically, every day of your life. The rest is magic.

True Colours
When was the last time you felt like you were giving far more than you were allowing yourself to receive? Without blaming outwardly, instead use your energy to look inward to find where this imbalance came from. Do so with love.

Freedom in Acceptance

Intention
True Freedom emerges when we see things as they are, and we don't attach a story around what is. We simply accept what is, remaining at ease and at peace with what is. This may seem impossible in the worst circumstances, but it will be the way through. Consider that acceptance is wearing a sweater on a freezing cold day. Why would you ever choose to go outside and let yourself get cold?

Reflection
Freedom is already yours. Have you been allowing it to rise? Look for ways to embrace what *is*, to lean into lessons without creating stories around what is. This is your power. This is your freedom.

True Colours
Where in your life are you experiencing some resistance about what is? What would acceptance look and feel like? Be specific in your discovery.

Feel To Heal

Intention

So often in life, we bypass, avoid, or dismiss our feelings. Especially the uncomfortable ones, the painful ones. Where do those feelings go? Do they show up in the body? Do they lash out at people who don't deserve it? Are they reactions that don't match the situation? This isn't about ruminating or dwelling on the past. It is about letting the feelings you didn't have the tools to work through before come to the surface now, so they can be felt and released.

Reflection

Feel the feelings that you have avoided. Do this by talking to a therapist, counsellor, a friend, a coach, or anyone you trust. Spending time in nature, meditating, journaling, or healing through breathwork. The feelings we avoid are typically heavy. You deserve to feel them, so they can be honoured and released, making space for more ease, peace, and joy in your heart and in your life.

True Colours

What feelings have you avoided, but you know are there, waiting to be felt?

Fear

Intention

When was the last time you did something that scared you? Can you lean into the things that cause you fear? Inquire about your fear? Allow for fear to become a teacher, to point you into the direction of your work, of opportunities for growth and letting go. Consider that, sometimes fear is just another form of excitement

Reflection
Fear can be your ally, pointing you in the direction of where there is healing needed; of where growth is available. The ultimate fear is letting love in, the ultimate freedom is choosing something fully.

True Colours
What causes you fear? If you asked this fear some questions about why it's there or what it might have to teach you, what would it say?

Self-Care Versus Indulgence

Intention
Have you considered the difference between self-care and indulgence? Indulgence will always feel good in the moment; this is why we typically indulge. However, that feel good moment will pass and you'll be left with the longer-term effect of the indulgence.

Caring for yourself will always bring you healing or growth, nutrients for your mind, body, and soul.

Reflection
Indulgence might feel like self-love in the moment, in response to the want or the perceived need. But self-care is the truest expression of self-love. It is the things you would do for a child or a loved one needing support, knowing it will make them feel good and will be good for them. It will make them feel held and safe and comforted. It will be things that fuel their health and well-being without regret or long-term effects that are counter-intuitive to true self-love.

Do these things for yourself, just like you would for a loved one: take a bath, put your feet up, go for a walk, talk to a friend, wrap yourself in a cozy blanket, drink water, read a book, eat nourishing foods, listen to music, and love yourself, truly.

True Colours
What did self-love look like for you today? What *can* self love look like for you today?

Intuition

Intention
In times when you disagree and say nothing, in times when you witness an injustice and say nothing, consider this to be a betrayal to yourself and your truth. Consider that through that dishonouring you are not embodying and respecting your role in this life. Your soul, your intuition, will always nudge you when it is time to speak. The nudge, the whisper, will feel uncomfortable, until it doesn't. You may feel a sinking in your gut, a flush of heat move through your chest, tingles. Listen to the cues and know that your intuition will never steer you wrong.

Reflection
Being true to yourself or to a cause, to social justice, may have consequences. It may be met with defensiveness or result in severed relationships. The other consequence will be a beautiful one, though: you will be honouring and aligning to your values and your truth. A consequence that will always create a deeper connection to yourself and the world around you. Your voice matters. What you believe in matters. You matter.

True Colours
When was the last time you listened to the cue of your intuition?

Possibility

Intention
Consider that your limitations are really found in your beliefs. Limiting beliefs. Get curious about what's possible for you today if you root for yourself, if you let yourself take up space, if you let yourself try and fail and try again.

Reflection
Work with yourself rather than against yourself. If not you, who? If not now, when? Life is fragile and fleeting; let yourself live fully and lean into the beauty of possibility.

True Colours
Removing all the reasons you can't or shouldn't, what aligns to your heart and becomes possible?

You Are Enough

Intention
The "not enough" lie is an epidemic. We walk through our lives with this feeling of not being enough. Not doing enough, not fast enough, not creative enough, not exercising enough, not reading enough, not eating enough salad. Not helping others enough, not being a good enough parent or child or partner. The list is a long one.

Where do you send yourself the message that you aren't enough? Allow that to come to your mind's eye. The undoing of this lie comes from within. Now, reverse the message. Whatever it was, affirm to yourself that you *are* indeed enough in this exact moment.

Reflection
In this exact moment, you are enough of everything. Internal dialogue contrary to this will only take up space, necessary space needed for growth, expansion, and the confidence to express yourself just as you are, fully and completely.

True Colours
What does your "not enough" voice tell you? Where was it born, from what experience or relationship? Talk to that voice and let it know the truth about your enough-ness.

Happiness

Intention
One of the top five regrets people have at the end of their life is "I didn't just let myself be happy." Sometimes we attach to all that feels wrong and forget to celebrate all that is right. Shift your energy today; shift the focus. Where thoughts go, energy flows. Choose to place conscious acknowledgement on the good, the beautiful, the blessings, the little things that make smiles wash across your face and bring warmth into your heart.

Reflection
This is *your* life to create. You are the artist, the creator, the designer of your life and your experiences. All of it. Knowing, in this work, that you are worthy of good things, why not create and design a life that is full of joy that you *allow* yourself to feel? The joy and happiness you feel won't be in vain; it will always be a contagious energy of love, light, and inspiration.

True Colours
Look back over the week. Where did you miss the opportunity for true happiness to flood through your body?

Good and Bad

Intention
I'm tired: bad. I'm happy: good. This is hard: bad. This is really easy for me: good. Rather than clinging to these notions, embrace the is-ness of all things without attaching a moral value. This practice of self-discovery lends itself to opportunities to expand, explore, inquire, and learn about yourself, in integrity with yourself, without judgement.

Reflection
Honour all the experiences on your path as authentic moments of truth. Sometimes, offering affirmations that you're exactly where you need to be; sometimes, offering guidance about where you can go and where you can grow. Experiences are just clues about how to deepen your relationship with yourself.

True Colours
When was the last time you were tired or sad and made it mean it was a "bad" or "wrong" feeling? Let yourself undo that now. Reassure yourself that you are human.

Making Orange Juice

Intention
If I gave you an orange and asked you to make six glasses of orange juice, you'd easily say no; with certainty, with ease. Not possible. Does it mean the orange is pathetic? Does it mean the orange is less of an orange? Or does it mean that it was being asked too much?
     When you are unable to say yes to overextending yourself, does it mean you are lazy and incapable? Or unskilled and unqualified?

No. It means one orange cannot make six glasses of orange juice, because it is simply and perfectly one orange.

Reflection
Be realistic about what is asked of you and respond with certainty and truth when you cannot do it all. The asker isn't responsible for asking just enough; you are responsible for accepting and committing to just enough, to what is possible for you in this moment and season of your life. You cannot do it all; you only have so much juice, because you are simply and perfectly one you. One human.

True Colours
Where have you stretched yourself too thin? Or where have others expected too much or you've expected too much from yourself? Reassure yourself that you are doing enough, that you are enough.

Putting People Above Us

Intention
We put people above us or below us within moments of meeting. This is a lie that will not bring us closer to equality. We must see each other as a reflection of the divine that is within all of us, as humans having a human experience, walking this earth, living this life. We have all been good at things, not good at things, felt sadness, grief, pain, joy, pleasure, fear, anger, rage, worry, loneliness, and love. We are human.

Reflection
See *your* true colours in others; recognize them and allow that recognition to bring you closer together and to let go of judgement. Get curious about their individual experiences. Inquire, listen, and learn. You are a powerful energy in the world. Yes, you. These are

the conversations that will build bridges, connecting and strengthening humanity as a collective.

True Colours
Who have you put above you, or below you? Where can you see yourself in them and dissolve the idea of separation?

Give Yourself Credit

Intention
Not to feed the ego, but to nourish the soul. When you read a book or listened to a podcast or attended a seminar and you declared, "It changed my life," it was true that those experiences were riddled with gold. This source of information was full of inspiration and valuable tools. But it is *you* who are doing the changing and the growing, utilizing the inspiration, the information, and tools. Give yourself credit and nourish your soul by paying the wisdom you have learned forward.

Reflection
Give yourself credit, then reveal and express your growth. Don't keep it to yourself. We are here to heal ourselves so we can help to heal others. When you believe in the lessons you are learning, that is what makes them powerful. Take time to live the lessons you learn, then make time to share the lessons you have lived.

True Colours
What words of wisdom, rooted in love, could you share with someone today?

The Quality of Your Energy Attracts the Same

Intention
Can you consider that you attract the energy that you emit? Invite this experiment for a few weeks, just to prove it to be true. Consciously conduct yourself purely with patience, empathy, and compassion, with a light and joyful heart, and notice the energy you attract. Also, notice the energy that you deflect when yours is pure of intent.

Reflection
You are a beautiful, bright, and powerful light. You have the ability to change the energy around you just by letting yourself shine.

True Colours
When have you absorbed the energy of someone else? When have you noticed your energy shift the energy of someone else?

Feeling Rushed

Intention
Are there times when you feel rushed, but you are moving slowly? Where you feel an energy of urgency in your body, in your chest and your heart? Notice this, inquire about it. Where is it rooted? When you identify the root, can you let go? Can you release it and let it move through you? Take a deep breath in. Exhale. Take another deep breath. Exhale. One more time, breathe in fully, let go completely. All is well. There is no rush, there is no urgency, you're exactly where you need to be.

Reflection
Notice when you are robbing yourself of the present moment. When you are feeling anxious or rushed. It's just an indication that you've put your energy into the future rather than feeling into the energy of now. It's just an indication that you need to take a few slow, full inhales and exhales. Placing full focus on your breath will always calm the sense of urgency and anxiety and it will always anchor you in the now. Trust your breath to ground you. All is well.

True Colours
When was the last time you feel anxious and rushed, even over-whelmed? How did it help? What did it teach you?

We Are Nature

Intention
When was the last time you extended the length and distance of your eye gaze? Created presence in what you see in nature? A tree, a cloud, the bright blue—or grey—sky, even a plant thriving inside your home?

Marvel at nature. Reconnect, stay connected with nature and all of her gifts that are part of you, too. You are part of a whole and complete universe. Remembering this will bring ease to your beautiful heart.

Reflection
Nature is us; we are nature. When we lose this connection, we lose part of ourselves. No matter where you live, there is nature. Look at the sky, set your gaze far beyond you. Stay there. Marvel, connect, breathe. Stay there some more and when you want to let go of your gaze, resist and breathe some more. Do this until you find peace washes over you. Invite that peace into your soul and take it with you, with presence.

Sinead Moylet

Invite this refuelling practice of breath and extended gaze in nature into your life, your toolkit of well-being.

True Colours
When you connect with nature, it stirs something inside of you. What does it stir? Let truth flow from your heart.

We Are Stewards of the Earth

Intention
We are stewards of the earth; however, we live in a society that tells us we are stewards of the *economy*.

If there is no earth, there *is* no economy. Our beautiful home, our only home, needs our collective and conscious stewardship. What can you do today to invite this role into your consciousness or deepen and expand your relationship with the role you've already accepted?

Reflection
We are inherently connected to land, water, to sun, moon, and sky. Tune back in, return to your true purpose in stewardship of loving the Earth as if it was your mother, because she is. Honour her. Make mindful choices one day at a time that grow and care for her. Decisions that don't hurt or deplete her. She is our mother; she is mother to our children and grandchildren and generations to follow. Love her for them, if not for yourself.

True Colours
In what ways have you acted in stewardship to the earth? What ways can you personally add to this critical role of humankind?

Third-Eye Knowing

Intention
Connect to your intuition. What is your relationship with your third eye? Your intuition, your deep and always-knowing? You've experienced this relationship, a "gut feeling" telling you something is absolutely right. A new home, a job, a relationship. Or that physical feeling telling you something is absolutely wrong, unsafe, or not meant for you. A right turn instead of left, a betrayal, or meeting a new person that isn't aligned to your values.

You've experienced resisting the intuitive cues you've felt, maybe ignoring them completely at times. You've also experienced the triumph of going with your gut without any other explanation, and it has led you further on your true path. Tune in today. Listen for the cues of your intuition.

Reflection
Nurture your relationship with your intuition. Deepen your connection so you can discern between fear and intuitive feelings. So you can honour your soul's journey by trusting that it knows where to lead you and will never fail you. Tune in by sitting, meditating, inquiring within and allowing the answers to emerge. Your intuition can be strengthened like any other muscle, simply by exercising it and allowing it to fulfil its purpose. Honour your intuition and you honour your authentic path.

True Colours
When did your intuition speak to you last? What was it trying to tell you? Write a commitment to turning up the volume of your wise and intuitive voice.

Grey Days Are Necessary

Intention
The grey days are necessary. They mean precipitation is building and release is coming. Rain comes and releases and nourishes all that is life.

Can you consider that we need to operate in the same way? Precipitation—emotion, sadness fear, frustration—builds, and it indicates a need to release, to purge through feeling, through the release of tears, releasing the energy attached to the tears. The tears, the release, and letting go nourishes the soul.

Reflection
Sunny days never feel so beautiful than after a few grey, rainy days. When you experience energetically grey and rainy days in your heart, remember that they always pass. Make time to feel your feelings on these heavier days. Release the precipitation from the energetic clouds and allow your tears to flow, just like the rain. The sunshine will always return, dear one.

True Colours
Recall a time when you felt low. Recall the transition out of the low vibration, how it felt, and what became clear when the clouds lifted.

Forgiveness

Intention
Forgiveness is a healing virtue for the one extending the forgiveness. How is forgiveness showing up in your life in this moment? Who do you need to forgive? Before thinking of others first, like you so often do, what about you? Have you forgiven yourself for all the times you accepted blame, because when things go wrong you assume

responsibility? You carry responsibility, sometimes without even realizing you're doing it.

Reflection
Notice the quiet whispers that tell you, *This is your fault* or *You did this.*, *You could have fixed this* or *You need to fix this.* As you would with your best friend, pause, breathe, and reflect from a neutral position. Is it really your fault? Is there accountability to be owned? If so, then okay, do what you must to rectify with another or resolve with yourself. But if it's truly not yours, allow that too, and inquire about the why. Why did you assume blame and responsibility when it wasn't yours? Love yourself harder. Sometimes, it's not your fault. It's not your fault. It's not your fault.

True Colours
What role is forgiveness playing in your life right now?

You Are Not Alone

Intention
The loneliest times of the human experience are times of pain, grief, sadness, anger. This is so because the pain happens when our hearts close. The energy becomes dark, heavy, paralyzing, and we quickly feel disconnected from others; sometimes even people who we love, people who love us.

Can you consider that we feel as a collective? We are all living the human experience, inclusive of suffering. There is nothing you feel or go through that hasn't been felt. Yes, your heart is yours; your grief, your sadness are yours. But perhaps it is time to open your heart in the face of challenging emotions and remember your humanity.

Reflection
There is comfort in numbers. In looking in the eyes of another when you are in your darkest moments and letting your heart, your pain, be seen. This will take energy, it will take an opening, and you *can* do this. Let love in; keep your heart, your most powerful energy centre, open at all times. Especially the hard times.

True Colours
Where do you feel closed and why? What would opening look and feel like?

Anticipation

Intention
Yesterday is gone. Tomorrow has not happened. Today, now, this moment, is what is real. It's the only thing that is real. Re-know, re-align to your personal power to feel into the now and to tune into the energy you are creating for your future.

Be the creator, and while you are creating, embrace and accept what is.

Reflection
Sometimes we feed the habit of giving up so much of our time energetically to anticipation of things to come. If we have something to do in the evening or the following day, we can spend the day in a state of waiting and anticipation. Hours of beautiful, precious time, gone.

Be here now.

True Colours
Where are you right now? Describe what is now: how it looks, how it feels, what is true and what is not

Let Your Troubles Wash Away

Intention

Let your troubles wash away today. When they arrive in your mind, let them tumble out from your body with each exhale. Through this, you will transform anxiety energy, worry, stress, and fear into a calm stillness within your heart. This is your power. Remember it.

Reflection

Your breath reminds you how beautifully alive you are. When the world troubles you, come back to the peace, the home within you. Nurture your soul with the waves of your breath and the beat of your heart. Your true frequency is serenity. Allow it.

True Colours

What troubles are you holding and what would it look like to release them? What would you need to invite in order to facilitate a true release? A conversation, a good cry, movement, action where procrastination sits?

The Polarity of Life

Intention

Can you hold space for the full spectrum of the polarity of life? To care deeply, but also to let go. To trust fully, but also to have boundaries. To apply effort but also invite ease. See where you can invite this paradox consciously into your heart.

Reflection

Trust the polarity of life. Challenges and fear are really just misunderstood allies. Challenge is truly just part of life's course load. Observe. Witness. Call in the lessons.

True Colours
Where is there polarity in your life today? Perhaps tired but happy? Sad but grateful? Explore this with your heart.

Spring

Intention
Spring is a wonderful reminder of how beautiful change can be. Where can you let go of the fear of change in the present moment of your life? Where can you let go of worry about change? Can you look to the lessons you've learned from the past and trust your tools? Know, from evidence of your past, that change brings growth and opportunities for you to get to know a whole new part of yourself.

Reflection
Let spring remind you of the beauty that can be found in change.

True Colours
What changes are you moving through right now? How can you reassure yourself or celebrate growth from changes of the past?

Mothers' Day

Intention
Celebrating the maternal, feminine energy in the world, wherever it's rooted and born from. That special kind of love that brings calm and peace to our hearts. The gentle touch, the open heart, the considerate and empathetic heart that expands and multiplies the energy and power of love around us. Extending and offering of this love that makes us feel safe and held, valued and nurtured to grow.

Whether you are a mother, a grandmother, or someone who embodies the feminine and maternal gift by smiling at children, making them feel safe and seen, you have contributed to a magnetic energy that is helping us on our quest to thrive. With love, with gratitude, with so much love, with so much gratitude.

Reflection
A celebration of every smile you've given a child, every embrace, every tear you supported to flow with freedom, every wild imagination you fueled with presence. You have given and received, and it has made a difference with reach beyond time and space. Today is dedicated to those you love and who love you.

True Colours
What is Mother's Day to you? If it's bright and joyful, I see you. If it's heavy and hard, I see you. Honour your truth. It is perfect. I love you.

Reprogramming Your Operating System

Intention
Reprogramming your operating system means letting go of the idea that having problems is a problem. Moving into acceptance of the lived experience, the human experience that unites us all. Where in your life can you simply accept what is? Discover a nugget of learning, of knowing and remembering.

Reflection
Consider that your relationship to situations is where your power truly sits. Get curious about the lessons being offered. Rather than attaching to the emotion wrapped around the situation, look for those lessons that are always there, waiting for you to uncover them.

True Colours
Where do you feel stuck? What learning is being offered that will allow you to unstick the stuck-ness?

Gratitude For Your Journey

Intention
Honour and extend gratitude for all facets of your journey. Can you sit in gratitude for the struggle you have endured? The hard times? The horrible times? If this feels absurd, consider looking at your past, at these experiences. You're on the other side of them, so it is safe. Sit quietly, look back as the witness. Look for the lessons that were offered to you, maybe even lessons you've already absorbed but haven't acknowledged in your heart.

Reflection
We look for the lessons in hardship, as the lessons are usually the ones we only need to learn once. If we miss the lesson or deny it, we may find the hardship returns in different forms, different ways. Our souls have chosen this exact journey to learn lessons and to grow, to expand and to deepen our ability to invite a blissful state of being. Seek lessons in all experience and you may find hardships themselves become easier to cope with. Rather than focus on the suffering in the hardship, you'll be placing focus on the opportunity for growth.

True Colours
What is the biggest, most significant lesson you have learned in life? How did this lesson come to be?

Connect To the Earth

Intention
Connect to the Earth. Take time, make time to ground yourself today. Place your bare feet directly on the ground. Bring awareness to the powerful energy beneath you. The offering of connection. As you inhale, feel and invite the magnetic energy being drawn up and let it be absorbed into your beautiful vessel, your beautiful heart and soul. Receive.

Reflection
You are a field of energy, transmitting energy. Replenish. Connect to the planet, to nature, barefoot and open to receive. As you inhale and exhale, enjoy this energetic exchange between you and Mother Earth. Continue in this way, breathing in and out, exchanging, replenishing, transmitting.

True Colours
When do you feel the most connected to Earth? The most connected to nature? Write about this, let it be poetry without judgement.

Truth Fuels Progress

Intention
Consider that progress speeds up when truth is the fuel. Healing speeds up, connection and authenticity too. Where do you need to set yourself free of the burden of carrying mistruths, half-truths, or lies? Small or big, know that they supress your energy and the energy of those around you. Let go of shame, step into acceptance, and let the truth guide your way through. It's faster this way.

Reflection
Your truth is your heart. When we deny what is true, we deny our heart. We diminish trust that truth is always the way. Love yourself enough to allow truth to emerge. Allow truth to take up space, even uncomfortable space. Find comfort in the discomfort and trust that on the other side of speaking your truth is freedom from shame, a deepening of love, and a strengthening of trust.

True Colours
Where is there a truth within you that needs to see the light of day?

Disappointing Others

Intention
When we worry so much about disappointing others, we risk disappointing ourselves. It's okay to make decisions that others might not understand or even support. You are here to walk your authentic path. Lean into what is right for you and your journey.

Reflection
You may disappoint others. Reconcile this in your heart, knowing that your choices and decisions are coming from self-love and an honouring of your journey. You can acknowledge the disappointment others are feeling and send them your love, while committing to what is right and true for you. Trust it all, even the disappointment in others.

True Colours
When was the most recent time you were aware that you disappointed someone? Was it rooted in an honouring of yourself?

Support Someone To Be Their True Self

Intention
Give someone you love permission to be themselves. Set them free
from people-pleasing ways. Notice when they are compromising
their truth in order to please another. Our energy is best protected
and nurtured when we are authentic. When we people-please, we
are looking for validation external to us. Look for validation from
within—it's the most potent validation you can experience.

Reflection
Be the energy you want to attract. When you exist in a space of
people-pleasing, you are dulling your energy and adopting the
energy of another. This doesn't mean their energy isn't beautiful; it
simply means it's not yours. The same goes for seeking validation
of your worth through people-pleasing. Validate yourself; you are
already so worthy.

True Colours
Is there someone in your life who you are trying to change? What
would it look like to encourage them to simply be themselves?

Happiness Is Our Natural State

Intention
Drop out of the reasons and the stories about why you aren't
happy. Happiness is our natural state. Bliss is our natural state.
Consider this as messages from the mind try to keep you playing
small. Replace those messages with gratitude for all that you are
in this moment, for all that you have in this moment. Look around,
inwardly or outwardly, and find five things that bring you happiness. Let one of them be yourself.

Can you simply *be* happy. Take a moment, take some breaths, see if you can energetically compose the music of happiness in your heart. You know how to do this; you have felt happiness before. Breathe and recall the feeling you know to be happiness. Allow it to wash over you, head to toe, inside and out. Perhaps you allow a smile, or goosebumps at the realization of your magical ways.

True Colours
What makes you happy? Let the list be long. Then make it longer.

Today Is A Great Day

Intention
Today is a great day. I claim it to be. Today I will be open to all the tiny opportunities for ease and joy. Today I will offer kindness to people around me. Today I will stay connected to my breath, my life force energy. This connection, this awareness will remind me to be here. Here is now, I am here. Be here now.

Reflection
Today was a great day. There were things that didn't go my way and those were great too. They allowed me the opportunity to find ease in spite of challenges. The beautiful parts of my day were clearer because I looked for them, like little treasures. My breath carried me all day long, into this very moment of peace, ease, and joy. I will take space now to breathe intentionally, expansively, and lovingly.

True Colours
What was today for you? Can you reflect on your day with a perspective of greatness? Looking at the parts that you overcame, the gifts, the blessings, the opportunities.

Go Inward

Intention
It is time to create a more inward life. Not a selfish life. An inward life where you tune into who you are, where you need to heal. What you can do to serve the greater good of humanity If, in these times, we continue to look outside of ourselves for happiness and joy, clinging to the idea that external forces bring us happiness, we will miss out on what is possible within.

Reflection
Create a life within. Create community around you. Look for ways to be of service, knowing small acts of kindness count too. The ripple effects a healed and conscious soul has in the world is the energy amplification we need for a more beautiful world to emerge. You are part of the change the world needs. Get to work, find your centre, find your peace, and come from love in all you do.

True Colours
The world I create within is contributing to the world around me. The world I am creating is...

Dreams With Fences Or Walls

Intention
Have you ever thought about the walls or fences you have unconsciously erected around what's possible for your life? Consider the limitless possibilities available if you let yourself imagine beyond the confinement of those fences. If you let those invisible fences dissolve. If you think it, you can become it.

Reflection
Reach farther, imagine wider, with no capacity or limitations, no walls or fences. Quiet the voice that keeps your fences up, defiantly telling you it's too hard, or what you are dreaming of is for other people, not for you. Lean into your heart's true desires and your imagination's dreams. Make a plan, then work the plan, mindfully. Your dreams are made to come true.

True Colours
What are you dreaming of behind the fences and walls?

Equanimity

Intention
Calm, connection, and equanimity (stability) are said to be the three qualities of a healthy mind. Invite those qualities into your day today, into your practices and rituals. If any of those are compromised, notice it, then take a moment and breathe.

Reflection
This too shall pass. When we truly awaken to the impermanence of everything, we become freer, lighter, more authentic, with the time and space gifted to us in every moment of every day.

Calm, connection and equanimity—keep these qualities in your mind's eye. Be calm with yourself and with others. Invite connection with loved ones and with yourself. Insist on equanimity, on balance in your life, finding the balance between effort and ease in all things.

True Colours
Where are these three qualities needed in your life or relationships? Plan to incorporate them mindfully.

Thanks For Understanding

Intention
When someone thanks you for understanding, doesn't that feel good? When we take time to sit with what another person's perspective or experience might be and what they may be feeling, we connect to a deeper sense of compassion and humanity. Sometimes we even recognize ourselves in the other person's experience if we drop the urge to judge or criticize. All we want as human beings is to be seen, heard, loved, and understood.

Reflection
We are so deeply connected in this human experience. Let's love each other harder, embrace our ability to come from understanding and to see and receive the offering of love that exists in being understood.

True Colours
Reflect on a time where you felt understood and what shifted inside of you. Where can you offer understanding to someone you love today?

How You Interact With Others

Intention
Consider that how you interact with others is how you interact with yourself. Are you authentic or pleasing? Avoidant or honest? Accepting or judgemental? Invite this observation, this awareness of yourself into your life and all of your interactions. Witness your interactions and reflect on them.

Reflection

How you show up in the world is where you choose to place your energy. Use your frequency and your powerful energy to fuel the vibration of authenticity, compassion, acceptance, and love. Do this in relationship and interactions with others and in relationship and interactions with yourself.

True Colours

How did you interact with yourself recently that was unkind and unsupportive? Remedy that with an apology to your heart and a promise to love yourself harder.

Take Responsibility For Your Internal Reality

Intention

In a world where we are bombarded with stimulus, disruption, activity, and noise, our minds become overactive and loud. Take personal responsibility for your internal reality by quieting down every day and becoming still. Stillness and quiet is what fuels the brain to optimize our capacity. We nurture resilience when we quiet down and go within. Take a few moments every day; create the habit, the ritual of quieting down. When there is disruption or discomfort, let yourself step into a place of peace and calm.

Reflection

Through the practice of stillness, we become clearer about anything we need to let go of. We become clearer about what we need to step into. We get to know our soul's truest desires with more clarity and authenticity. Send gratitude to your heart, with your heart, for inviting the practice of stillness into your day, every day.

True Colours

Today my internal reality is... No judgement, no fixing, just truth.

Conversations With Your Soul

Intention
Invite conversations with your soul. Ask this truest part of yourself what am I most proud of... most afraid of...what do I forgive myself for...

Acknowledge what is true, without judgement. Journal, discover, ask questions. The more we actively deepen our relationship with ourselves, the more self-love will flow with ease.

Reflection
When you step into a conversation with your soul and allow honesty and emotion to guide all of your answers, you release what's not serving you and you are able to celebrate the work you've been doing. Deepen this relationship with yourself through using all the lines on a page. Use quiet moments to yourself to authentically spend time with yourself. Strengthen and cherish this relationship and notice the shifts around you, because of it.

True Colours
Today my soul wants to tell me...

Gifts Within the Darker Moments

Intention
Can you sit with the idea that in the darkest moments is the most powerful medicine? Can you trust that the triggers, the pain and disruption are pointing you to the exact place where healing is needed?

Reflection

When darkness emerges, keep your heart open. Send love to the intensity in your chest, the heaviness in your heart. Nurture the darkness as you would a small child. Not bypassing or stuffing down, but allowing it to flow through you, knowing that with acknowledgement and compassion, it will pass. It always does. Ask the darkness why it's there. Continue to ask questions until light permeates the darkness with beaming love and absolves all of the pain.

True Colours

What does darkness feel like when it greets you? What does it need, what is it typically asking for? How can you give love to yourself through those days?

Choose Things That Align With Joy

Intention

Make choices from your highest place of excitement. Choose all the things, big and little, that align with pure explosive joy! Eating the juiciest, dripping peach and relishing in the beauty and nourishment it's infusing into your body. Leaning into the thing you'd love to do, but you've allowed fear to be the decision maker. Ask yourself in all of your choices: Is this coming from my highest place of excitement? Notice the answers or alternatives that might surface when you inquire.

Reflection

What would you do today if you were making choices from your highest place of excitement? If nothing comes to mind, sit with it. The choice doesn't have to be monumental; it just has to be authentically exciting. Dropping all fear, anxiety, all the language of "but what if." Drop the examination of all that could go wrong and allow excitement for all that could go right flow through you with the bliss you were meant to embody.

True Colours
What would joy say to you today? What would it tell you to do?

Choose Your Regrets

Intention
Christopher Hitchens said, "Choose your regrets." Choosing your regrets is a different approach to ensuring you are living a life that is truest to your heart's desires. Would you regret going to the yoga class or regret not going? Daily decisions and big decisions. Would you regret staying in the job or seeking something truer to your joyful self? Consider the path with no option for regrets when you sit with your end-of-life self. Rather than overthinking the details, lean into your soul's truest desires, and trust the rest.

Reflection
Choose your regrets. Would you regret having the needed conversation or regret not having it? Would you regret trying something new or regret not trying? We deserve to live this life in bliss, and bliss happens when we listen to the truest desires of our heart and soul. What comes to the surface for you when you invite this sentiment?

True Colours
What regret can you empower yourself to choose in your life right now? Sit with this; it can be a mind bending reflection.

Sinead Moylet

Are You Living In The Now?

Intention
Are you enjoying and living in the now or worrying about, planning for, thinking about the next thing? When we are in that state of being, what happens to "now"? The now becomes missed because we are giving it away to things that have already happened or things that haven't happened yet. We miss the beauty, the goodness, the blessing and wonderment of right here, right now. This moment. Let go of all the stories and the worries and simply live with presence.

Reflection
In these times we need to lean deeply into love with all we have. We can't be effective in this effort if we aren't present for it.

True Colours
With no elements of the past or the future, what does now look like? What does now feel like?

There Is No Separation

Intention
There is no separation. We are all connected. If you are healing, I am healing. If am healing, you are healing. This healing journey we are all on, whether we choose to see it and experience it or not, is so much bigger than we allow ourselves to believe. The ripple effect of your healing spreads far and wide through your energy as an energetic being. It inspires without you needing to try.

Reflection
Your healing, the energy of peace and love that you cultivate on your healing journey, spreads far and wide. Why? Because that's how much your energy matters in this world.

True Colours
Think of something you have healed from and how your healing positively impacted someone you know.

Take A Moment To Breathe

Intention
Take a moment to breathe. A moment to stop in your tracks when you notice the mind is taking you on a roller coaster you don't want to be on, a roller coaster you do not want to choose. Breathe. Look around. Notice. Take a moment to breathe consciously every day. To fill your lungs with peace and ease, to exhale the disruption that doesn't allow for peace and ease. To look up at the vastness of the sky and let it remind you of the vastness of you.

Reflection
When things feel small or constraining and restrictive, remember your vastness. Breathe deeply, set your eye gaze far in the horizon, and let your exhales expand your loving heart. Do this and notice what you feel.

True Colours
Breathe in and out. Slowly. Slower. Do this for a while. What was achieved?

Healing Active Wounds

Intention
Set the intention of healing. Active wounds make us do things, say things, and choose things that don't align to our truest soul journey. Our soul's journey is about finding and following your joy. Active wounds are a barrier if they're not looked at and healed. You aren't what happened to you. It was an experience. Sometimes a dreadful, horrible experience. It caused wounding. The wounding is not yours to hold onto. The lessons you might be able to extract from the wound are yours to discover and hold close as a stepping stone to loving yourself harder.

Reflection
Imagine what it would feel like to let all of the stories go, all of the experiences that caused wounds you didn't deserve and that weren't your fault. Sit with that question and listen to the gentle sense of peace and calm that washes over you. This is the state of being that you deserving peace and calm, through the healing you deserve.

True Colours
What wound is active within you today? How is it showing up? What does it need? Remember, as you reflect on this, you are not your wounds.

Creating A Life From Within

Intention
It is important to remember to create a life from within, not feed the programming of creating our life from the outside, the external, the system. Give yourself full permission to slow the brain, the mind, the body, and simply breathe. Take these moments, perhaps an hour, as a retreat from all responsibility. Let go, let be. Let the medicine of stillness do what it knows how to do. Trust.

Reflection
Let all the stress, the worry, and cycling fatigue completely melt away. Let yourself transcend deeply into the mind. The quiet place, beneath the noise, where all is always well.

True Colours
When you imagine a place within you that brings absolute peace, what do you see?

I Am

Intention
It is a great time in the world to replace the negative with the positive in all things. To do this, consider a practice of mindful awareness every time you begin a sentence with "I am." I am tired, I am not doing enough, I am not good at that. We do this because we have been conditioned this way. Our work as human beings in changing the energy of the planet is to change the energy within us. Changing the affirmations we choose. This morning, affirming: I am mindful, I am kind, I am compassionate, I am worthy, I am enough.

Reflection
"I am." Your existence. You being here. The simple truth of "I am" is enough. Remember the power of these two small but mighty words. Every time we begin a sentence with "I am," we affirm the rest to be true. We give it our energy as truth. Become aware of this; witness yourself. Remember your power to choose; choose to replace negative affirmations with positive ones. Your new truth will be fed and fuelled by you.

Try it: I am important. I am loved. I am enough.

True Colours
Write "I am..." and then claim all that you are and all that you desire to be as if it's already happened.

Embody Peace

Intention
Sit with the word "peace." Right here, right now, gently close your eyes for a few breaths and allow the word "peace" to repeat in your mind and in your heart. Good. Now notice the energy you invited as you sat with the word and the intention of peace. You did this.

Can you invite the polarity of being at peace while managing noise, challenge, or disruption? Choose peace today. Let it lead the way, let it have a voice in all of your thoughts and conversations.

Reflection
Know that who you are is much bigger than any fleeting circumstance or disruption; bigger than any disagreement or challenge. You've seen this over and over in your life and yet we still let it take away our peace. Next time there is noise of any kind, let yourself handle it with a peaceful heart.

Healing Reflection 1: You are Worthy

of Healing Your Heart

"Normal" is simply defined as "what we are used to." So, many of us have gotten used to living with the pain from our wounds, our trauma, from grief. We have accepted our pain as our personal "normal."

But you are here, reading these words, to change that. Because your heart knows better. The true essence of you, your highest self, your beautiful soul, is saying no This will not be my normal anymore. I want more. I want to shed the layers of pain, sadness, anger, grief, fear, worry, anxiety, and stress.

Before I shed these layers, I understand that I have to let myself feel these feelings. To hold space for my heart, I must honour my wounds, honour my truth. I must acknowledge my wounds, acknowledge my truth. For so long, I have pushed these feelings down, hoping they'd just melt away. Looking at my pain is hard. Sometimes, it even scares me.

It scares me to feel the grief because it's so big. It scares me to feel the sadness from the times I was belittled or dismissed or betrayed. It scares me to feel the sadness from the unjustness and unfairness I have witnessed. The unjustness and unfairness I have experienced. It scares me to look back at the very big feelings my little-self had, with no one to help me through.

We cannot change what we don't acknowledge. Our wounds and our traumas have changed us. They have dimmed our light. They have erected walls in fear of hurt happening again. They have made us live in constant worry that our children will experience what we have experienced.

Our wounds have changed us. Anger brewing, bubbling inside, sitting at the surface, ready to lash out at those who inadvertently pick at the scab of our unhealed wounds. People who don't deserve it. Our wounds have us living with constant chatter in our mind. Criticizing ourselves in ways we'd never criticize someone we love.

None of this is your fault. Our pain keeps us playing small, feeling unworthy of pure, true, healed love. It lies to us, telling us we are unworthy of the purest, truest, healed happiness. Our pain keeps us believing on some level that a life of underlying sadness is normal.

In this work, you're letting yourself discover a new normal. You're letting yourself finally feel it all. Loving yourself enough to hold space for your feelings to be felt so that they can be released. The grief from missing loved ones who have passed, the pain from relationships ended, the pain from betrayal, from abandonment, from tragedy. The frustration that comes from living in a society that tries to convince us that life is just hard. The avoidance of feeling it all, fully, has been all-consuming.

You have wished it away, hoped time would heal. You've smiled so much, hoping to convince your heart that you're fine. You've tried to pray it away. Now things are shifting. You are in the real work of self-discovery and healing. It's moving through you, right now, because you are showing up for yourself in a whole new way. Showing up for your heart, for that little version of you who finally gets to let it out and cry.

You deserve to discover a new normal. To get to know the healed version of you. To step boldly, bravely, lovingly into the *truest* version of you. The you, the authentic you that has always been there. The you before things happened to you. The you who wants to *live* this life, unattached to stories and experiences. The you who will live each day with a lighter heart, wearing a smile that is in complete charge of your heart. The you who roots for yourself, reminds you how worthy you are of good things. How worthy you are of happiness. The you who reminds you that you *are* good enough, that you are *enough*.

Become the truth of you, that knows you are not defined by how hard you work, or how much money you make, or how many people like you. The truth of you knows that this life is fleeting and it's time to celebrate and *see* all the beautiful little gifts that are right there, every single day. You are reconnecting with the you who is optimistic, joyful, playful, curious, easy-going, kind, and loving.

You are returning to the authentic you who first arrived in the world. Keep showing up for yourself, for those around you who see you, who love you. Keep stopping the cycle of pain. Keep leading with love.

Say these words out loud as a claiming of your truth:

I am letting go.

I am loveable.

I am healing.

And so it is.

Being in Stillness

Intention

The practice of being in stillness gives us access to the wisdom found only in stillness. Let yourself marinate in this daily. Observe the experiences that emerge in stillness and allow those experiences to be your teacher. Notice, am I trying to escape the stillness? Am I fidgeting, resisting? Let those observations guide your work, without letting judgement creep in. Progress happens with practice of stillness, not our judgement of how "good" we are at it.

Reflection

Honour and revere the energy of stillness that you collect. Becoming your own witness is easier when you invite the practice of stillness into your soul's journey. You're a greater teacher than you give yourself credit for. Allow stillness to give you the evidence of that.

True Colours
Be still. What did stillness say to you?

What Does My Higher Self Want
to Say to Me Today?

Intention
Begin today by asking, "What does my higher-self want me to tell me today?" Before writing, take some slow, deep breaths to let go of the thinking mind. Allow the pen to move, without thinking. It will feel like you're making it up, but this is you, connecting with the highest version of self. Listen to this voice; it knows you best.

Reflection
Your higher self is not your personality. It is the part of you, the essence that was here before you were born, and the essence that will be here after your physical self leaves this world. This voice wants you to live in peace, joy, and bliss. Begin this conversation with your higher self every single day, whether it is in writing, journaling, or meditation. Perhaps it's frequent consultation in moments of decision. "What would my higher-self want me to do here?"

This is the voice that will always guide you with love. Your higher self is waiting for this initiation from you. Some of us go our whole life without engaging in a relationship with our higher self. Let this relationship flourish by giving it your time, space, and energy.

True Colours
What does your higher-self want to say to you today? Listen closely.

Gratitude

Intention
Make a connection between gratitude and the idea that "this too shall pass." It's not as gloomy as it first appears. This concept, this intention, is about realizing that "this too shall pass" is true for both the good and the challenging times. We try to sit in deeper gratitude for the small blessings and the fleeting moments of joy. Then we try to apply gratitude for the challenges of life, extracting the lessons and growth opportunities with that same gratitude. Trusting that here as well; this too shall pass. Let yourself be joyful and grateful in the face of it all.

Reflection
This too shall pass. Ride the waves of life with ease and deep gratitude. Allow love and joy to lead you through it all. This is your power.

True Colours
It all passes. The ups, the downs, the days, the nights. Write a note to yourself to remind yourself to take it all in waves of acceptance and presence.

We Have Forty Thousand Neurons In Our Heart

Intention
We have forty thousand neurons in our heart, neurons that are capable of knowing intuitive truth, like a second—but underutilized—brain. Call in today a deep remembering of what the human species' authentic design truly was. That we are feeling beings who think, not thinking beings who feel.

Reflection
The thinking mind can sometimes sabotage us with its protective nature. We gave it the relentless job of worry and protection when these things paralyze us and keep us from moving forward, creating a barrier to our intuitive knowing. Remember and trust the power of your beautiful heart to guide you. To answer the question, "What would love do?"

True Colours
What does the wisdom of your heart want to tell you today?

Your Energy Frequency Is Like a Radio Dial

Intention
What you tune into will be found. There is a lot of information and negative vibration coming at us in these times, more than ever before in history. We will find greater energetic fuel in grounding ourselves, dropping into our hearts and asking the mind to quiet down, just be in this moment. Tuning out and tuning in.

Let yourself find retreat from the outer world. Let go and let be. Allow the medicine of this practice to do what it knows to do.

Reflection
Be devoted to your wellness. Stay calm and peaceful in these times as much as possible. Let the natural human state of peace and serenity emerge often. This is the truth about our power to change the energy of the world around us.

True Colours
What frequency did you tune into today and what came back?

Awareness Is Simply Paying Attention

Intention

Simply put, consciousness is awareness of what is happening in your mind, your heart, and your soul. Awareness is simply paying attention.

Sitting in the seat of your own witness, paying attention is how you arrive in a place of consciousness. Walk through your day, every day, as if you're watching your thoughts. Look for patterns of unkind words or criticism that you'd never offer to loved ones; notice them before attaching to them as truth. Then, simply replace them with what is true: that you are showing up as the best you can, and that is always enough.

Reflection

How we think and the thoughts we attach to make up our reality. Remember that this means you are the creator of your reality. You can choose your thoughts, you can quiet the ones that are not kind, that aren't helpful, and you can replace them with thoughts and words that are kind and are helpful. Be your own best friend in every moment of the day and notice how good it feels to root for yourself and deepen the friendship with your soul

True Colours

How can you root for yourself today? A pep talk perhaps.

Personality

Intention

Our personality is a pattern of how we think, how we act, how we feel. Knowing this, acknowledging it, is a reminder that we are fully in charge of our internal experiences and our response to the external experiences. Remember your power to design the pattern of your personality.

Reflection
If you want something different, do something different. Change "I can't" to "I can." Consider how greatness would live today. Design your life through every thought, every feeling, every behaviour. You are the creator of your personality.

True Colours
Be truthful without being critical. Is your personality creating patterns in your internal world? Where is there opportunity to shift patterns that aren't serving your greatest good?

We Are In A Spiritual Revolution

Intention
There is a spiritual revolution happening in the world right now. You are contributing to it by being in this work of self-inquiry and by taking good care of your energy. Perhaps you notice more people having conversations around spirituality and consciousness, acknowledging that we are all connected. Remember that you're never alone on this journey. Don't lose sight of the energetic impact you are having by being in this work. Take a moment to celebrate and recognize your efforts, even on days when it hasn't been that easy.

Reflection
Recognize yourself. Acknowledge your efforts. Acknowledge that you have learned to look into the shadow parts of yourself, and it hasn't been easy. Even when it wasn't easy, you explored and uncovered the root of your pain and faced it head on. Each time, every uncovering, every self-realization making it easier for you to stay

on the path of self-discovery and healing. You should be proud of yourself, and if this is hard to feel, tune into your highest self and you'll feel pride and love wash over your beautiful heart.

True Colours
Look back at the version of you that was ten years younger. How have you grown into your spirituality?

The Beauty of What Is

Intention
Recognize the beauty and wonder of what is. Sometimes we get caught up in wanting more, in being more, being better, having more. Consider that in conversation with your future self, perhaps in five years from now, you might be met with a version of you who wishes there was a greater sense of appreciating where you were in *this* very moment of your life's journey.

Whenever we are in a place of wanting, we are refusing and rejecting what is. Wanting points to lack and forgets to realize the blessings already very present. Today, allow yourself to cultivate and adopt a mentality of recognizing and celebrating what is.

Reflection
In this moment, you are perfect. In the next moment you will be perfect too. Love yourself truly and relentlessly, in every moment of every phase and stage of your life. Notice the peace that envelops your heart when you do this. Exhale. You're exactly on track and perfectly on time.

True Colours
Look at what is right now. What parts have you overlooked, that deserve acknowledgment or gratitude?

Master Your Breath And You Master Your Mind

Intention
In this very moment, take a slow, full inhale and a long, slow exhale. Do this five times.

When you were breathing you thought, *I am breathing in a long breath and breathing out slowly?* You weren't thinking about what you need to get done later, tomorrow, or next week. You weren't thinking about what went wrong yesterday. You were here, in the now, the only place that is real, in the experience of your breath. Thus, you trained yourself to calm the activity of the mind. Whenever you tune into the now and into your breath, your thoughts will quiet down just like a puddle after the storm stops. This is bliss.

Reflection
Breath is a tool that helps you surmount life's toughest challenges. Breathing with intention creates endless vitality. It strengthens the lungs, giving oxygen to the brain. It revitalizes every organ in the body. Give breath your time and attention every day and in every experience of disruption or uncertainty. Breath itself is mindfulness.

True Colours
After five slow, very long breaths, what did you feel?

Resistance Is Wasted Energy

Intention
Consider that resistance is a waste of your *valuable* energy. Resisting what is, what is happening, what you *are* experiencing, creates unnecessary suffering. Your energy can be better utilized by simply moving through the experience with true presence and acceptance. This is part of your free will.

Reflection
Whatever you're avoiding stays with you and it will take time away from moving through your journey in a way that cultivates growth. There are things we don't want to experience, certainly. But not wanting an experience won't change it. Use your valuable energy to look at the experience from a higher-self perspective. Seek the lessons, the opportunities, and know that like all experiences, this one does not define you, and it will float by just like they all do. Just like they always have.

True Colours
What are you avoiding on your journey? What part needs to be looked at or accepted? What will shift if you do?

Movement Has Been Given
Higher Value Than Stillness

Intention
Movement has been given a higher value than stillness. If we let it, the mind will always manifest more to do, to think of and worry about, because we rarely practice stillness. Today, invite a practice of stillness, perhaps some yin yoga or meditation or simply sitting still. Trust the void, the space between words and activity and the silence between thoughts.

Reflection
The unfolding of life is an inside job. Align to the life that was made for you by being aware of your frequency and taking care of your energy as if it is separate from you. Nurture your energy in periods of stillness and notice what happens to the unwanted patterns in your life.

What did stillness say to you today?

Expansion and Contraction

Intention

Change includes contraction and expansion, highs and lows, growth and letting go. Just like nature is in constant change, so are we. We are nature. Rather than resisting change, let yourself accept the journey of constant transformation, knowing that in order to grow, sometimes we have to let go. In order to grow, sometimes there is contraction or discomfort we must experience. Try to shepherd yourself through this ever-changing life with compassion and grace. Why would we choose anything else?

Reflection

Like the outer layer of bark on a tree, we need to let go of what is confining us, or not meant for us, in order to make space for growth. This is an uncomfortable but reliable process. Let yourself find comfort in the discomfort of change and growth. Let yourself trust the journey of the soul, and that your highest self is always rooting for your growth and evolution. Let yourself love yourself through it all.

True Colours

Reflect on the last time you experienced contraction that was followed by expansion and growth.

The System Wants Us To Rush Ahead

Intention

The systemic world around us wants to keep us rushing forward, keep us feeling like we can't keep up. We see this in the retail world with Christmas decorations for sale in September, Halloween candy sold in August. Constantly looking ahead so we don't spend needed time examining the here and now. These are the times when our practice of mindfulness becomes challenged. Can you protect your energy and your inner peace in these times? Not letting the hurriedness energy tell you that there's anything other than right here, right now.

Reflection

Find moments to dwell in stillness. To remind yourself of the here and now, of peace and quiet. Know that it is as critical as movement in this lived experience. Become centred in yourself in the face of the pull to the outer world. Be at peace and remind yourself of your ability to slow life down to a pace that is kind to your heart.

True Colours

How much of your thoughts are on things that need to be done or what's coming next? Reflect on this without judgement but with loving acknowledgement.

You Give of Yourself So Often

Intention

You are giving of yourself so often. Let today be an exercise in coming home to you. Let your intention today be...*you*. Acknowledge yourself, any energy you need to move and release. Maybe it is unhelpful energy born within you that you need to release, or unhelpful energy you've absorbed from people or the world around you. Feel all the feelings you need to feel so that you can make space in your heart for peace. You are safe; you are held.

Reflection
You are where it all begins, always. There is no greater gift you can give yourself or the people in your life than to process what you must. To let go and free yourself of anything not supporting love, joy, peace, growth, and balance. Our intention today was *you*. Because you matter, so much.

True Colours
Simply affirm, "I matter, so much."

Let Yourself Live In Deep Joy

Intention
The truth is, joy is the most challenging state for us to be in. We habitually go to worst case scenarios or live in a land of but-what-if's, sometimes waiting for the other shoe to drop. Witness this in yourself and catch it before it takes hold, before it becomes a story you attach to. Remember that living in full joy is a choice.

Choose a quality you want to invite more of in your life in order to realize greater joy. It could be balance, wisdom, strength, forgiveness, abundance, love. Whatever emerges when you inquire within. When you have chosen a quality that aligns with you, let it complete this phrase: "I am ____." Write it down, repeat it, commit to its truth.

Reflection
You are the one who manifests your own destiny. Use the power of belief to be whoever you want to be. To let go of what *won't* bring you closer to the truest, most vibrant version of you. Use the power

of affirmation to create whatever you want to create. A joy-filled life; a joy-filled way of being isn't for other' people It is for you.

True Colours
What quality will bring you more joy? Incorporate this into a daily affirmation practice. Affirmations take some work to embody as habit, but it won't work unless you do.

Stillness The Teacher

Intention
Stillness is a great teacher. It teaches us to invite acceptance about what is. In our lives we have experienced hard things, hurt and discomfort. Sometimes, we choose to avoid these uncomfortable sensations and to busy our minds with other things. Sometimes listening to a small voice that tells us we aren't worthy. The present moment then becomes so hard to embrace, whether it's joyful or difficult. In stillness we stay in a motionless state, where only the presence remains. Invite moments of stillness, perhaps even a stillness practice, into your life.

Reflection
The choice to be still, to be present in this life, takes great courage. To stay in feelings of discomfort and to be present for the growth being offered. To stay in peace without hurrying toward the next thing. To love yourself enough to spend quality time with yourself in stillness, nurturing discomfort or celebrating joy. Be still and be present for all stillness has to offer.

True Colours
Be still. What softened in stillness? What became clear?

Choice

Intention
We have so many opportunities for choice in our lives. We can choose to find ease in the dis-ease or comfort in the discomfort. We can choose to respond to challenging people with kindness, because we choose to believe they know no better, or they are leading from their wounds. We can choose to listen to our gut, our intuition, and strengthen our sense of inner knowing every time we do. We can choose to believe the universe is out to get us when things go wrong, or we can choose to believe the universe is conspiring for our best interest and things going wrong are blessings in disguise. All of the choices we make are either rooted in fear or love; low self-worth, or powerful self-love.

Reflection
Empower your ability to choose, and to see how much more peace you can bring into your life when you realize that choice is present in every moment of every day.

True Colours
What did you choose today? Is there a choice that would have given you greater peace?

Start Today By Loving Yourself

Intention
Start by loving yourself today. Become connected to yourself, dropping out of your head and into your heart, where love lives. Acknowledge all that you are, all of your gifts and beauty. Keep walking this path of self-love, even when it feels challenging, and don't let the love you have for yourself be conditional. Journey

inward, to your heart, your truest self, underneath the experiences and noise, every day.

Reflection
Aren't we so good at telling people we care about how to care for themselves? Now it's your turn. "I am open to all that the universe and my life's journey holds for me. I will comfort myself and wrap myself in a blanket of love and hope. I will make room for my heart, in my heart, for my life, in my life, for love, tenderness joy and exhilaration. I will take gentle, loving care of me. Those around me, will always benefit, too."

True Colours
Does loving yourself come easy? Does it take work? Doesn't it make sense to love yourself? Look at all you've faced and overcome.

Lessons From Birth

Intention
On our birth journey, we leave the warmth, safety, and peacefulness of the womb and begin a painful, restrictive, perhaps even scary journey into life. This journey doesn't come with the advance knowing that the discomfort will result in our growth, in being held and loved; we just have to trust it.

If this is the very first human lesson given to us, why do we disregard it? Creating more suffering every time there are challenges, restrictions, or discomfort. Instead of trusting it all with a deep, primal remembering.

Ah, I see; I am growing.

Reflection
Can you come back to the very first lesson you learned when you entered the world? Trusting that growth is always on the other

side of challenge and discomfort, without fail? Our birth journey reminds us of this.

In the midst of all the uncertainty and discomfort around you, maybe you can find greater ease by considering that there will be growth on the other side of it all. Allow a growth mindset to be available to you today.

True Colours
What feels uncomfortable about life right now? Can you consider that there might be growth on the other side of this uncomfortable experience?

Embodiment of Enough-ness

Intention
"I am not enough" It is one of the biggest collective lies in the human experience. We walk through our lives with this feeling of not being enough. Not good enough, not smart enough, not doing enough, not fast enough, not helping enough, not attractive enough, not special enough...the list goes on. Consider that the origins of this internal message, this lie, came from outside of you. But the undoing of this lie *is* your responsibility, and it comes from within. Filter thoughts of not being enough and replace them with validation that you *are*.

Reflection
The truth is, you *are* enough. One of the top regrets people have at the end of life is that they didn't let themselves *be* happy. Start with this practice of self-validation to prevent that from being *your* regret at the end of *your* life. Undo the lie. You are enough. Let yourself be happy.

True Colours
Aren't you tired of feeling like you're not enough? Then let it go. Talk to the parts of you that feel like they aren't enough. Ask them where they came from and give them the love they need to let go of this untruth about you and your worth.

Saying No

Intention
Tune into your own, internal guidance system, the energy that emerges when you say yes or no to something. Listen for intuitive hits, a sense of certainty or peace when you make a decision. Let go of justifying your "no" with all the reasons you can't or won't. Simply, lovingly allow for a no.

They don't always need to be big and devastating or disappointing; sometimes they are simply an honouring of yourself. Feel your body's response to the question in the moment. Be open to what it's telling you and deliver a no as lovingly as you'd deliver a yes. Practice this today, tuning into when your body is speaking to you, guiding you.

Reflection
Tune into your truth and then allow for a commitment to self, to your truth. Saying no, cancelling or rescheduling, or simply not being available, doesn't make you a bad person. Be witness to these critical thinking patterns and soften. Your body, your internal guidance system, has a voice that wants to be heard and wants to be trusted.

True Colours
So often we forget to listen to the cues of our body. When was the last time your body gave you an answer that you listened to and acted upon?

Still Letting Go of "Good" and "Bad"

Intention
Let's invite our collective letting go of "good" and "bad" as we strengthen our ability to fully own and accept our experiences. Rather, embrace the is-ness of all things without attaching a moral quality to them. Life lends itself to opportunities to explore, to grow, and to learn about ourselves. The learning is best realized when it's done without judgement.

Reflection
Honour all the experiences on your path as authentic moments of truth. Not good, not bad, just truth. Sometimes offering affirmation, sometimes offering guidance. They're all clues about how to deepen your relationship with your truest self.

True Colours
What did you once label as a "bad" time in your life that you now see was actually working for your greater good?

Energy Transformation

Intention
Are you conscious of your power to transform energy? Have you taken the time to acknowledge yourself when you do this? You transform energy when you have a challenging conversation and you choose to sit in silence or meditation after. Or when you feel overwhelm consuming you, so you put on a "guarantee dance" song and you move, shake, and release. When you have a busy day that perhaps has left you feeling depleted, and you go to your yoga mat to move your body, or answer the call to be in nature, to walk and process. All of this is the transformation of energy, and it's your

superpower. Transforming "I can't" to "I'll try" or "It's hard" to "It's challenging." Look for opportunities to transform energy today.

Reflection

We can choose to attach to and be consumed by energy that drains us and depletes us. Or we can transform energy that doesn't serve us into something that fuels our hearts.

True Colours

What unwanted energy do you feel today? Notice where it sits in your body. Transform it now—you have the tools—then reflect on your experience.

The Best We Can

Intention

The best that we can do counts. Sometimes, especially when there are parts of life and the world around us that we know need fixing, healing, or repairing, we get frustrated with what's possible in our personal realm of influence. Some days the 'best we can might feel like it falls short of what we would like to be able to do to help make a difference. Consider that doing the best that we can, with what we have, always makes a difference. The energetic contagion of your efforts is felt far and wide, whether you're aware of it or not, and you are making a difference. Thank you.

Reflection

Peace starts at home. Within. Doing the best you can to make a difference in the world is enough. Whatever that looks like—donating clothing, food, protesting, advocating, supporting a child or a neighbour in your community. Layered on top of that is your contribution to peace. How do you contribute to peace? By simply creating peace, within.

True Colours
When you extend a smile to a stranger, it's a contribution to peace in the world. Don't overthink this. Reflect on how you can or will contribute to peace with a conscious heart today.

Inner Peace Is the Key That Opens the Door to Outer Peace

Intention
Meditate. Invite a sense of passiveness, of letting go, giving your mind and your body a break from the energy of effort, of doing. Drop into the energy of passiveness, acceptance, and ease. Let your inhales be slow and steady and your exhales be long and smooth. With each inhale, imagine fresh, nourishing oxygen entering every cell of your body. With every exhale envision any worry, tension, or stress you are carrying leaving your body. Give yourself permission to balance heart and mind. Breathe, become witness to your breath, and be still.

Reflection
Inner peace is the key. If you have inner peace, the external problems—the noise surrounding you—cannot disrupt your sense of tranquility and bliss. Take this balance of heart and mind with you and out into your life.

True Colours
The goal isn't happiness, it's peace. It's through peace that true moments of happiness can be felt. Where can you allow for more peace today?

Your Thoughts In A Catalogue

Intention
Imagine your thoughts were listed and you could choose them as if they were in a catalogue or a file. Categories, optimism, encouragement, compassion, gratitude. Wouldn't that be amazing? The good news is, you can. The categories are there, not only for you to choose from, but for you to design. Try this today; notice what shifts.

Reflection
You are the designer, the architect of your life. The external will challenge you with this, but the truth never changes: you can change your experiences by changing your thought patterns.

True Colours
Catch yourself today when thoughts emerge from categories you don't want to align with. Do this with mindful intention and reflect on how it went. Then do it again, tomorrow and the next day, and all your days ahead.

Our Mind Reflects Our Life

Intention
It is said that a cluttered space means a cluttered mind. Consider that it goes both ways: how we keep our minds is a reflection of the life around us. Consider firing your mind from trying to solve everything. Find the balance of accepting what is with all that you want to change. Cultivate this energy of acceptance with self-love, knowing that loving yourself is the energy that will inspire those around you.

Reflection
In times of challenge or feelings of discomfort with all that is happening around the world and around us, cultivate self-love. Wrap your arms around yourself, take a long, hot soak in the bath, take a walk in the woods, take full, beautiful, and nourishing breaths, and love yourself first. Taking care of your mind and the thoughts you allow will show up in life and the experiences around you.

True Colours
What clutter fills your mind today? What thought patterns need to be tidied up or dissolved?

Watch The Things You Think, Just Like A Movie

Intention
When we witness ourselves, observe our thoughts, it gives us the opportunity to coach ourselves. It gives us the ability to come from a place of self-worth and undo thought patterns that hurt us or lie to us about our worth. Be the witness to your thoughts and notice how much more self-love emerges when you do.

Reflection
Witness the moments when unkind thoughts come into your mind. Quickly release them and replace them with loving thoughts filled with compassion and empathy. Thoughts that remind you of your worth, your value, and all that is possible in this beautiful and fleeting life.

True Colours
Where do your thoughts keep you playing small? Where do your thoughts take you to places that don't even exist? What is your relationship with your thoughts? Acknowledge this with love, not judgement.

Happiness can sometimes be a Choice

Intention
Happiness is not by chance, sometimes happiness is a choice. Exercise choosing happiness relentlessly. Remind yourself that peace and happiness is our natural state of being. The noise, the shadow in the world, will always be present, but your happiness can be too. Allow a wash of happiness to flow through you and around you right here, right now. Perhaps fueled by a joyful memory. Call it in, allow it in, welcome it in to stay.

Reflection
Pursue happiness.. Invite it into your life and your heart every day. When happiness overflows, let it flow and spread to others. You are powerful and you are a radiant bright light, who makes the world a happier, more beautiful place just by being you.

True Colours
Get excited about life! Even if life feels heavy and unfair in this moment. Get excited about what's possible. Reminding yourself anything is possible, because you are an absolute miracle. Write. Reflect.

Criticism Can Only Hurt When You Believe It

Intention
Criticism can only impact you to the degree that you believe the criticism to be true. When you're exposed to judgement or perceived criticism, ask yourself, is it true? If the answer is no, then let go. If the answer is yes, then simply move into self-inquiry, a conversation with your soul, and resolve the issue with and through self-love. This is your journey to design and uphold.

Reflection
Get acquainted with criticism and feedback. Accept the power you have to change what you don't align with. Accept that there are those who may not see the real version of you. Choose this acceptance by choosing to love yourself, even when others don't, and even when you notice a part of your shadow that you need to bring into the light.

True Colours
Think back to a time where you received criticism that hurt. Without re-living the hurt, without attaching to it again, reflect on that experience and explore where the uncovered lesson might be.

Let The Beauty Of Your Heart Be Revealed

Intention
Is it challenging for you to let the beauty of your heart be authentically revealed, authentically expressed? Is it challenging for you to take up space in this way, letting your gifts be known? Consider a world where each of us lets the gifts of our heart and soul shine brightly and unapologetically. Not from ego, but from love. You are here to shine and to let those around you see and be nourished by your bright light.

Reflection
When we doubt or question our gifts, we deny the truest essence of who we are and who we came here to be. Notice when you feel this energy coming up and let the voice of your inner best friend get loud! Repeating to yourself, "I have gifts, I have value, I matter, I am a bright and radiant light."

True Colours
What gift do you have that you have difficulty claiming? Reflect or write, and claim that gift now. Claim the way it makes you feel to own this gift that is all yours, waiting to take up more space.

The Disease To Please

Intention
Do you suffer from the disease to please? Tune into your true and pure intentions, your motivations for doing something for someone else. If your intention is to be accepted, to be loved, to be known as kind and saying yes when you want to say no, you are abandoning yourself. You cannot live an authentic life without disappointing some people, sometimes. And that's okay. Say it with me, "That's okay." Being true to you is the path forward, the path that becomes smoother every time you honour your truth.

Reflection
Heal from the disease to please. Take the journey through yourself, to yourself by getting curious when you say yes, even though you'd rather say no. The people truly rooting for you in this life will not feel disappointed. The people who are have their own agenda; you've disappointed their ability to fulfill their motivation. People who always want you to honour you will see you and love you more for being true to your beautiful heart.

True Colours
Who are you trying to please lately? Why? What can you learn? What can you shift from?

You Are A Student Of Your Life

Intention
You are a student of your experiences. Always look for the lessons, the wisdom being offered through your experiences and the experiences you witness in others. We are here to grow, to heal, to discover and uncover. We are here to end cycles of pain, of trauma, of unhealed hearts. This is the truth about our soul's journey, and the essence of who we are.

Reflection
There is no such thing as failure. It's just here to move you in another direction, the direction meant for your highest good. Pause and look for the lessons; collect them like treasures and rely on them to guide you next time guidance is needed.

True Colours
What is the biggest lesson you have learned in your journey so far? How has it ended a generational cycle? Big or small, they all count.

Mindful Moment

Intention
If you're always thinking about another time and space, you are never really living. You are missing and giving up on what is real. You're missing the now, where most often, all is well. Use your breath to find concentration. Give your mind a job to do—"Watch my breath"—in and out and in and out. My chest and belly rise and fall, in and out, in and out. The breath moves through my nose, through my mouth, in and out, in and out. This is now, this is peace.

Reflection
Breath is the bridge connecting mind to the present moment. Use you breath to take hold of your mid and to embody the now, where all is well.

True Colours
Is mindfulness something you practice, visit, or embody? Where can you apply more mindfulness this week? Make a loving commitment to yourself.

Surrendering Is Not Defeat

Intention
Surrendering is not an act of defeat, backing down, or weakening. Surrendering is not authorization, it's not permission. Surrendering is a claim to your personal power. A release into what is and to who you are and what you are moving through in this very moment. Surrendering is the humility of being human, it is power over the ego, it is letting go of suffering. Surrendering is where peace lives. Where can you surrender today?

Reflection
Let yourself surrender to what is. Surrender to acceptance. Surrender to the love within you and around you, to guide you and surrender to peace.

True Colours
Where can or has surrendering allowed space for peace?

Retreat From The World

Intention
Take an hour to retreat from the world and come back to yourself. Let your breath guide you into a deep, meditative state. Let your breath guide you deeper into yourself. There is nowhere for you to be but right here, right now, floating just above consciousness. The world can feel heavy and chaotic, so coming home to the beautiful place that is your body, your centre, is necessary. You are always a safe space for you to return to.

Reflection
Keep tuning into the soft, smooth rhythm of your breath. Feel your aliveness, your vibrancy, your beautiful breath, and your powerful heart beating in your chest. You are allowed to set the heaviness of life down for a while. Return to the simplicity and energy of your aliveness.

True Colours
An hour! Did you do it? How did it feel? Was it difficult or liberating or a bit of both? Reflect.

Hold Space For Yourself

Intention
Hold space for yourself for the next little while, not letting the space be filled or crowded with anything else than messages from your heart. Hold space for the whispers of your body and heart to be heard. Hold space with the consciousness of your breath. Hold space without judgement or interpretation. Hold loving, nurturing, compassionate space for you, from you.

Reflection
Hold space for yourself to process life's experiences. To reflect on and tune into how you are doing in this very moment. Hold space to listen for the whispers of your body and the whispers of your beautiful heart.

True Colours
You hold space for others. Hold space for yourself for the next five minutes. What did your heart and soul have to say in this space you held?

Warrior

Intention
Can you embody your inner warrior and laser-like focus of your yoga practice throughout your day? Can you be deliberate and disciplined in every step, every thought, every breath?

Can you be so tuned in and true to yourself that you listen for and answer the call for rest? So tuned in that you have awareness of your potential, and when you can do something that the old voice used to say you couldn't? You have been a warrior in this life. You have overcome and gotten to the other side of every challenge you have faced. Today, celebrate and expand your inner warrior.

Reflection
Warriors rest; they reflect, they breathe, they challenge themselves, they turn compassion inward. You are a warrior in the most expansive expression. Take time to acknowledge this in your heart and to remind yourself of this when challenge knocks at your warrior door.

True Colours
How have you been a warrior in this life? How were you a warrior today? How can you be a warrior tomorrow?

Doing Versus Being

Intention
There is a push and pull between doing and being. There are parts of our life, of our practice, that require action and doing. There are parts of life of our practice that require stillness and being present for now. Notice where you can be present for it all and let go of the need to fill time and space with thoughts, with "waiting." When we bypass moments of stillness without feeling into them, we only cheat ourselves out of the sweetest moments of this life.

Reflection
In the moments when you have nothing to do or nowhere to be, rather than inviting guilt and a list of all you "should" be doing, lean into and relish in the sweetness of stillness and find comfort in just being.

True Colours
How do you connect with stillness, with being?

Integration

Intention
How do you integrate what you learn about yourself, on your mat or through your experiences, into your life? The belief is that how you show up on your mat is how you show up in life. How you show up in challenging times is how you show up in all things. Witness yourself today, without judging, just observation, noticing. The rest is magic.

Reflection
Whenever we practice becoming our own observer, we learn about ourselves. We integrate lessons like staying instead of fleeing challenge. We learn to breathe when things get hard. We learn to be mindful about how we are treating ourselves and the language we use. We learn to root for ourselves and lift ourselves up when we fall. Breathe, find the balance between effort and ease, compassion and rest, and invite kind, encouraging self-talk into your heart. Become your own best fried; you'll never lead yourself astray.

True Colours
What are the lessons you have learned—on your yoga mat or in challenge—that you take with you out in your life? What did you notice about yourself today in how you showed up? Without judgement, just noticing.

Magnetism

Intention
You are magnetic. The thoughts you think, the beliefs you hold, your thought patterns you attach to as truth, will all attract and draw in energies and experiences to validate these stories of the mind. This is truly our work as a collective: change any patterns and stories that are not serving your greatest good and taking up space where joyful, loving energy can live.

Reflection
What you seek, you shall find. Notice where stories in your mind are patterns of self-sabotage or pessimism. Notice how they don't align with this future version of yourself that you are creating so mindfully. Then simply let them go. Invite thoughts, beliefs, and patterns that will act as a powerful magnet for the most beautiful life you can imagine. Acknowledge the shifts as they become known to you.

True Colours
What thought patterns are you ready to let go of? What thought patterns do you want to create to be a magnet for your greatest life?

Fear

Intention
What is your relationship to fear? Instead of letting your fears be wrapped in negative, shadow energy, can you befriend them? Get to know them, ask questions, and get curious about them and where they are rooted, where and when they develop. Small fears, big fears—notice when they surface and get curious about what they might be able to teach you about your journey and letting go.

Reflection
All of our emotions invite a deeper connection, a more expansive relationship with ourselves, if we honour them and get to know them.

True Colours
Get to know your fears. Ask them questions about what they are trying to tell you and from what experiences they were born. Come back to this inquiry often. Reminding yourself in this work, that you are safe.

Love

Intention
Imagine if the whole world operated from love. What would change, what would shift, what would become possible? Change in the collective begins from change on an individual level. If we all take responsibility in leading from love, the world will be a kinder more peaceful place. Let love guide you. You'll know its voice because it will be void of fear.

Reflection
Anchor yourself in love. Let love guide all of your thoughts, your decisions. Heart-centred energy is the future; it is currency. It is what will propel us forward in our collective evolution. Allow yourself to embody and express love in all of your days.

True Colours
What is your heart telling you today? Tune in, drop down, and listen for its message.

Presence

Intention
Presence can be found by getting into our bodies. Lay on the ground or on a mat. Can you be here, fully here with your breath guiding every moment as you make shapes with your body and explore what's possible? Being fully present is always the most challenging part of this practice, of living this life. But, like anything that we want to get good at, practice with true devotion and progress will meet you.

Practice makes progress. Send gratitude to yourself for your practice of mindfulness. Send gratitude to your body that does so much for you, without you even having to think about it or ask. Take some slow, thoughtful breaths. You are so held.

True Colours
What were the most present moments you allowed for today? How did it feel?

Community

Intention
There is an urgent need in the world for healing, for community and belonging, as our collective mental health has been challenged by events over the last few years. The powerful and peaceful energy you feel in community is because of you.

We talk so often about how the energy we put out is the energy we receive in return. That by cultivating our peaceful, joyful, authentic energy, we contribute to a ripple effect of peace, joy, and authenticity in the world. So today is a celebration of you. You belong so deeply and lovingly to our global community.

Reflection
Remember that by simply existing, you are enough. Let this knowing be the gateway to connecting with and building community with confidence.

True Colours
Where has a sense of community helped your growth journey? Where can you increase or spread the energy of community in your life?

Breathe

Intention
During the days of back to back appointments, meetings, celebrations, or tending to the needs of others. During moments of life when it all feels like it's moving faster than you can, find your breath.
   Remind yourself that you are doing your best and that your best is, in fact, good enough. Send an invitation to your heart, through your breath. An invitation to let go of tension, to dissolve useless stress, and to remind yourself that you are doing better than you've been letting yourself think.

Reflection
Breathe amidst the busy-ness. Breathe to bring your mind peace. Breathe to drop into your heart and into your body. Breathe to remind yourself that this moment, this inhale and exhale, is the only moment we know for sure. Breathe to remind yourself what matters most: you here, breathing, alive and well.

True Colours
Take five slow inhales and exhales with your eyes closed. How did that feel? How will you create space for mindful breathing every day?

Trust

Intention
Trust that you are right where you need to be today. Trust that you're exactly where you are supposed to be in your life, even if there are parts of life that feel unsettled. Let your breath anchor you, support you, guide you toward trust and acceptance. Through all your joy, through all your challenge and pain. Let your breath

be your most trusted, reliable tool. Let your breath be your most trusted, reliable friend.

Reflection
Breathe in and breathe out, like little sweet love notes to your heart. Like messages of validation, reassurance, and support. Breathe in and breathe out, using this tool you have full control over, to let go of everything out of your control. Breathe in and breathe out and allow the calm it brings to soothe you in all your days to come.

True Colours
How is your relationship to the powerful tool of your breath changing you?

Being of Service

Intention
Being of service is the greatest expression of your healing journey. It propels your healing forward with a beautiful, love-filled momentum. Service reminds us we are all healing, we are all walking this path together, just at different stages and phases. If you see someone falling behind, walk beside them, remind them they are not alone.

The healing you have worked so hard for and continue to work so hard for has the ability to illuminate the path for others. Being of service will nourish your heart.

Reflection
If you see someone falling behind, walk beside them. Remind them that they are not alone. If you see someone left out, include them. If you see someone struggling, remind them you, too, have struggled. If you see someone doubting themselves, remind them that you see them. Being of service doesn't need to be organized or planned; it can exist in tiny moments, all day long.

True Colours
How were you of service today, yesterday, this week? Remind yourself of the ripple effect of your love.

Simply Be

Intention
Of all the "I-have-to's" today, let "I have to simply BE" move to the top of the list, taking priority over all else. We operate from a place of busy-ness as a collective, from the conditioning of our social structures, when it's truly not our natural state. Today, let all of your troubles wash away. If they arrive in your mind, notice them and let them fall away with your exhales.

Allow your practice, your movement today, to transfer any worry, anxiety, or fear you are carrying into faith, calm, and trusting energy. Take the energy that softens your heart with you and leave the rest behind.

Reflection
Remind yourself, "Sometimes, I have to simply be." You are so beautifully alive. So beautifully here. When the world troubles you, when life presents challenge, come back to the peace, to the home within you. Nurture your soul with the waves of your breath and the beat of your beautiful heart. Remember, your truest frequency is serenity.

True Colours
What does "just being" look like for you? Is it challenging? If so, write about why. And consider this: like anything else, practice makes progress.

Being Known

Intention
Our intention today is to let your heart be known. We have all closed our hearts at different times in our lives. We close down, shut out, erect walls of protectiveness around our heart. This happens when we let our mind lead the way. The heart does not want to close.

Tune more deeply into the voice of your heart, and let it lead the way, through feeling your feelings, honouring your truth, and keeping your heart open.

Reflection
Keep your beautiful heart wide open! Let love and joy be in charge, and when pain is present, sit with it, honour it, let it flow through your heart without staying there..

True Colours
Where have you put walls around you heart? Why did you build them? Can you take those walls down by writing about your experiences and honouring your feelings fully?

Power

Intention
Feel and know your individual power, simply by virtue of being human. Celebrate all the powerful ways you show up for yourself and all the powerful ways you show up in the world. Acts of kindness and generosity, empathy for others. Being inclusive and seeing and celebrating our differences. Being one step ahead of your thoughts. Knowing how things will turn out if you react in a certain way, and then course-correcting to create an outcome that brings forward a more loving, useful experience.

Reflection
This morning, celebrate your powers in your practice and in your life. As you move and breathe today, let it feel powerful. Fill your powerful cup!

Power is energy. Take care of and celebrate your energy and you will strengthen your powerful ways.

True Colours
What were your powers today? How did they show up, and how did you see them and utilize them with purpose? Powers can be found in both innocent, fleeting moments and in big, expansive gestures.

Compassionate Inquiry

Intention
Knowing your triggers and where they are rooted is where your power lies. Noticing the moment, the *very* moment you feel that trigger pulled, that disruption in your heart, the physical sensation of it. Pause, breathe, witness, instead of attaching and reacting. What story is coming up right now for me? What lie did this trigger activate? What wound did it open? That I don't matter? That I'm not good enough? That I'm not worthy of love or that I'm not loveable? Whatever it is, it is pointing to the direction of healing through feeling. Once you've identified the lie, replace it with the truth.

Reflection
Take time to feel what you need to with compassionate inquiry. Identify the lie your wound is telling you, feel what you must, and replace the lie with the truth. Do this over and over and your wounds will ease. Triggers will be ghosts of the past.

Sinead Moylet

True Colours
Trust the triggers to teach. What trigger have you experienced recently? Write and explore with compassionate inquiry.

Breaking Free

Intention
Break free from conditioning accumulated in old systems and social structures. Not a heavy task at all! It's okay, you're not in this task alone.

Reclaim yourself, the part of you that wants to see and feel peace and harmony in the world in this lifetime. We are guiding in a new era of heart consciousness, the truest signature of humanity. Do this by reclaiming your ability to create a peaceful and harmonized experience every day, every opportunity. In your immediate surroundings, add the word "friend" to all of your interactions. To the cashier at the grocery store: "Have a good day, friend." Or by offering a hug to someone you sense is needing it. Trust your sense! This too is a reclaiming. We are custodians of heart energy; embracing this truth of our collective power will make a difference.

Reflection
We are laying the necessary groundwork, the foundation for a whole new way of being. Doing this not by placing all of our attention on what's falling away, but by fuelling heart energy and guiding in the new. This is a new era of loving consciousness that will bring us back to the truth of who we are.

True Colours
How have you expanded your heart today? How did you share the energy of your heart and how did it feel?

Mind Versus Heart

Intention
We have lived in a deep system of conditioning that didn't allow us to connect our minds and our hearts. All of that is falling away now and we are ushering in a new era of heart-consciousness. An era of love, peace, and harmony that we so long to see strengthen and replace old ways and systems. It might feel impossible some days, especially if you listen to the news. But this is the truth of the path we are on.

Take a big inhale and drop into your heart on the exhale. Stay there.

Our greatest sadness is when our heart isn't acknowledged by others or by what we witness in global actions. We feel it. The missing part of humanity. The good news is, all the discomfort, all the falling away of old systems, is a sign that we are making way for new.

We may not see heart energy every day, but we can live within it and fuel it's fire as individuals. Choose all your words and actions from love. Help others to feel safe in their heart centred emotions. We are custodians of heart energy, and the more of us that embrace this truth about authentic humanity, the faster we will heal as a collective.

Reflection
Take a big inhale and drop into your heart on the exhale. Stay there. Lead from there, think from there, feel from there, speak from there, love from there. This is the currency of the future, and your heart-strengthening work leads the way for others.

True Colours
How do you connect with your heart when your mind noticeably dominates? How do you exercise strengthening your ability to lead each day from the heart?

Meeting Yourself

Intention
Meet yourself, as if for the first time. Notice the qualities you admire, the quirks that make you smile. Notice the energy you emit and the love that shines from your heart. Use this practice of stepping outside of yourself to witness all of your goodness and strength. To give permission for admiration within. It's so important to carve out intentional time to come back to these practices where we slow down and pay those regular visits with ourselves. To check in, to acknowledge, to love. To deepen the quality of kindness and compassion we give to our minds, our bodies, our heart and soul.

Spend this time with yourself, lovingly.

Reflection
Today, you spent time with you, in loving awareness. You distanced yourself from the voices of the world so you could hear the voice of your heart and meet yourself for the first time, with admiration

True Colours
When you quieted the noise today, what came up? What did the practice of meeting yourself feel like?

Caring for Your Energy

Intention
Emotion is the energy that moves everything forward. Love connects and unites. Fear keeps guards and walls up. Hatred divides. This is why taking care of our energy and emotions today, in these times, is so important. A priority, with none higher. Our emotions, our energy today signals to the future, creates the future. Taking

care of your energy today will guide you to where you're supposed to be, living the life of your wildest dreams.

Reflection
Silence, mediation, feeling your feelings. These are three ways to take care of your energy that will invest in the creation of your future self. Take care of your energy like the sacred battery that it is. What you charge with that battery will depend on the degree of care that you give your energy.

True Colours
What investment did your energy make today? How will you or how did you care for your energy today?

Letting Go

Intention
Let go of struggle on repeat. Let go of doubt about yourself and your path. Let go of giving your power away to people and experiences that don't serve your highest self or your greatest good.

Invite trust in yourself and your journey. Invite trust that struggle can be shifted into ease when we believe in the growth being offered. Invite expanded self-worth. Invite turning your dreams into reality. Let go, to make space for the invitations of your heart to be met and fulfilled.

Reflection
Abundance in all things is a process of letting go, making space, and believing your worth to live in the space and experiences of your heart-centred creations.

True Colours
What can you let go of today? What will it make space for?

Sinead Moylet

Manifestation

Intention

Henry Ford said, "Whether you think you can, or you think you can't—you're right." This is the truth about manifestation. It's about embodying all that you are desiring in this life as if it's already happened.

As you do this, avoid the feeling of "wanting." Every time we want instead of desire, we are feeding energy of lack in the present. Instead, know that you are worthy of whatever it is you desire. Call it into your life. Feel the feelings of the good things coming and enjoy the energy that fills you when you do. Why not? Believe, envision, and remember that simply because you are here, you are worthy.

Reflection

Manifestation is believing and embodying everything you say after "I am." I am worthy. I am attracting good things. I am loved. I am enough.

Get excited. Imagine and embody the feelings that will come when your desires are fulfilled. Ask for what you desire in life and do little things every day that will support the creation of this future version of you. Remember, simply because you are here, you are worthy.

True Colours

What do you desire? What can you get excited about, what can you *let* yourself get excited about as if it's already happened? The thinking, analytical mind has no say here. Write from the heart.

My Journals

These are the journals into which I poured my healing work over the years. These pages contain the lessons, emotions, intentions, and reflections you will move through in the pages of this book. I wrote for me; I share for you.

My Writing Spot

Tucking myself away in a room for a week in small-town Fergus, Ontario, above the Brewhouse pub (no Irish jokes), to transpose thoughts from my journals into my manuscript was deeply nostalgic and offered the quiet I needed. My family had a trailer nearby where we would spend weekends and summer vacations for years, my favourite part of childhood. I could have done better by myself for the ergonomics though. (Thank you, yoga.)

Me & Sarah

Sarah is five here, one year after my mum passed away (at fifty-nine years old). Sarah had just recovered from double lung pneumonia, where she almost lost her life; she would be diagnosed with Type One Diabetes shortly after this photo. Like I said in my dedication, she's my hero. It is 2024 now and Sarah is twenty-three and thriving. She has a gift for childcare work, and is a talented artist, amongst many other gifts.

Sarah, twenty-two, looking magical. Letting her True Colours shine.

True Colours Original Painting

On Mother's Day, 2018, Sarah gave me this painting, into which she poured her creative soul. The image on the front of the book is a version of this original. The painting is titled "True Colours"—of course.

Slow Down

Intention

Give yourself the time and space to slow down. Slowing down restores your energy. Restored energy helps you to think more clearly. When you think clearly, your reality becomes clear and awareness of your blessings begins to re-emerge.

When your reality is clear you will become more aware of the whispers from your heart and the whispers of the universe guiding your path. Sometimes, we need to slow down in order to speed up.

Reflection

We are human BEINGS. Give yourself the permission to slow down and BE, even if it's just the slowing of a busy mind. Clarity is the gifted side effect of slowing down. Becoming clear on life's blessings that are truly all around.

True Colours

When you slow down, what clarity emerges for you?

Healing Reflection 2: You Can Be Your Own Hero

When you find that voice within that says, *I want something better for myself*, you become your own hero. When you decide not to shrink yourself to make others comfortable, you become your own hero.

Your past included experiences that you assigned meaning to. Most times unconsciously. Meaning about your worth, your enough-ness. Even meaning that you had failed. But the meaning you assigned came from the pain, not the truth.

The little you who was told not to cry, the you who was left or who had needs that simply weren't' met. The you who faced horrible, unbearable loss. The you who has carried the weight of the world on your shoulders, as if all problems are your fault and everything that goes wrong is yours to fix.

Tell yourself it's okay. You can cry, you can absolutely cry. You need to cry. You being left or having needs unmet was about what the other person was carrying or refusing to look at, not about you or how much you matter. Let those parts of you, carrying so much, know that the weight of the world is done being carried by you, and it would appreciate very much if you would put it down. As you put it down and feel the relief and the lightness, you will see none of it is yours to fix.

Your work is to love yourself. To love yourself so hard that hugging yourself comes with ease. To let go of criticizing and shaming yourself for the parts of you that have lived from pain, that did things from pain, made choices from pain. Replace the criticism with permission to be. To live fully. Permission to be soft and opinionated. Permission to let love in. Permission to try new things and to lean into the wonderment of life.

It's okay to be different, to be you. You represent the variety that can be found in honouring the human experience. So lean in. Lean into life all the way. Lean in so fully that you need to and get excited about getting to know this new, beautiful, truest version of you.

Because you are here, you are enough.

You don't need to prove this to anyone. It's already true.

You are capable.

You are gifted.

You are unique.

You belong.

You can walk through life without the heaviness. You can walk through life without the overwhelm. You can walk through life freely, by quieting the tapes and the narratives, the untruths that live in your mind. Replacing the voice that says, "Play small" with your new voice that says, "Take up space." You are on a journey of freedom and healing that is what the universe wants for you in this very moment.

Pay attention to the sweetness of life, the small things that bring you joy and delight. Sunsets, laughter, silliness, playfulness, trees, clouds, community, love, donuts. Moments of love and moments of awe and adventure. Life. It's all yours.

Say these words out loud as a claiming of your truth:

I deserve to heal.

I deserve to be free from suffering.

I am worthy of a joyful life.

I am creating my future in this very moment.

I am making space for peacefulness in my heart.

I am loved.

I am love.

And so it is.

Presence

Intention
Let the tool of presence go with you today. Use this tool with quiet reflection, inviting moments of time and space to seek and be present for the energetic gold life has to offer. Presence will give way to your awareness of the truth of your abundance.

Reflection
Time can move quickly if we forget to be here. If our minds are spending all of our time either in the past or in the future, we miss out on now. The past is gone, and the future hasn't happened. Be here for the now, and don't miss the experience of being here now. When you do, you miss the experience of life! Take time with you.

True Colours
Can you notice when your mind takes you to the past or the future? If you quiet down and return to presence, what do you see? What becomes true?

Seasons

Intention
As seasons change, you may have feelings of disorientation coming to the surface. Depending on the season, perhaps there is a greater sense of schedule or obligation, perhaps the pressure to have as much fun as you can. Tune into your heart in the coming days and weeks and acknowledge any sense of disorientation that arises. Allow it to simply be. Continue self-care and self-love, grounding into yourself. Invite stillness; you are in this very moment.

Reflection

Sometimes, it is through disorientation or getting lost that we discover new things that we might otherwise not. This journey is about trusting it all, even when it's disorienting.

True Colours

When have you felt disoriented recently? What did you find, discover, learn about yourself? Perhaps you haven't inquired about that yet. Write freely and the lessons will emerge.

Doing Nothing

Intention

The art of doing nothing. The power of stillness. The subtle release inside and out that comes through the doorway of stillness, taking you a tiny bit deeper in every moment. The need for stillness is greater than ever. This because the hours in our day spent in action are greater than ever. Let yourself settle into doing nothing, to being idle and calm, and savour the experience of complete stillness in your mind and body.

Reflection

When you are still, you assert your worthiness to be still. Through stillness you find your way back to the essence of you. When we make stillness a part of our life, when we invite the balance of yin and yang, we strengthen inner peace. We expand our capacity to experience life in balance, in gratitude, and in harmony.

True Colours

When you choose to do nothing, what does your inner critic say? When you choose to do nothing, what does your inner best friend say?.

Protecting Joy

Intention
Think of the most recent time someone's love lifted you up. That's because love is a contagious energy. The energy of love is the currency of the future. There is a bit of an energetic pull-though, a battle on the planet between controlling/fear energy and heart/peace energy. Try not to let this get you down. Try not to let it jade you or shift your focus. Trust that heart energy will rise and override, if we keep contributing to this shift. Do this by remembering your inner world is yours and yours alone to create.

Reflection
Be a protector of joy and love on the planet. The energy of love and joy has the power to diffuse so much! We protect it by becoming it.

True Colours
Is it challenging to witness the energetic battle on the planet? Take some time to acknowledge that challenge. Then take some time to lift yourself up and acknowledge yourself for what you bring to the change on the planet. Don't look for grandiose examples. You know by now that all change helps.

Move Slowly

Intention
In our current society we have unconsciously associated a negative energy with the word "slow." Moving slowly or that taking a break means we are struggling or becoming weak. Today, consider a new way of being that has been lost in the crazy tempo of modern life. Consider that success can be measured by how much and how

deeply we invite quality rest and restoration. Allow yourself intentional and purposeful time to experience rejuvenation.

Finding balance, creating and asserting time for your restoration, is a gift to yourself, to the people and world around you.

Reflection
Move slowly, mindfully, consciously. Rest when rest is called for, perhaps even offering yourself rest before it's called for. The more mindful and rested we are, the more beautiful life becomes.

True Colours
What does "slow down" look and feel like to you? How can you make a commitment to your heart to offer rest before your body asks for it? What would that commitment look like?

Spring Equinox

Intention
The spring equinox greets us. It is Mother Nature, planet Earth's new year. A special time where there is balance between lightness and dark. New beginnings, new growth, new life. A time where we let go of darkness and welcome light. A deeply transitional time where we can invest some thought into setting intentions for the season ahead. What do you want to do more of? What do you want to do less of? What do you want to learn more about? When new growth begins in nature, we can align to this energy of growth. We too are nature, after all.

Sometimes growth isn't about learning, it's about unlearning. Sometimes it is as simple as shedding any low vibrational energy that built up over winter. Take a few moments, some slow, calming breaths, and begin to invite the energy you'd like to embody this spring.

Reflection
Spring equinox is a special time of balance, to plant seeds of all kinds for new beginnings and growth. To remember your ability to grow, to change and adapt. To take up space with your beautiful heart.

True Colours
What intentions do you have for this spring? What do you want to learn and unlearn? What do you want to do more of? Less of? Honour what's true for you, without judgment.

Full Moon

Intention
Full moons are times of transformation. An opportunity to invite the emergence of your truest self. This doesn't just happen without our participation. Through cleansing and clearing and purifying, you make space for this emergence.

Today, get into the deep corners of your body, your heart, your mind, your soul. Allow yourself to soften ad release energy that may be occupying space that could be used for the growth and expansion of your highest self. As you do this, you will notice sensations; sometimes positive, sometimes more intense or uncomfortable. Look at these sensations as weather patterns, not attaching to them with any sense of permanence. Your work is to allow, allow, allow.

Reflection
Allow. Let go. Make space and repeat. Be receptive to the light you are inviting into your mind and body through this full moon energy. You held space for clearing and cleansing. Aligning to the enormous energetic powers of the full moon. My wish for you is that the space you create is filled with all the intentions your heart desires.

True Colours

What did you find in the corners that you were ready to let go of and release? What have you made space for? Notice sleep pattern changes during the full moon and be tender with yourself. Drink extra water and love yourself hard.

This Too Shall Pass

Intention

A truth that is so hard to believe when you are in the middle of "this." So, whenever you find yourself feeling stuck and attached to permanency of a challenge, remember all of the "this" you're already on the other side of. All of the "this" in your life that did indeed pass.

Reflection

This too shall pass. The "this" does pass. It always does. When the clouds clear as they always do, you'll have light, wisdom, and strength that you can take with you, so the next "this" isn't so hard.

True Colours

What "this" are you in right now? Write and reassure yourself that this, too, shall pass. Acknowledge some of the "this" you've already gotten to the other side of.

Honouring Your Feelings

Intention

When you honour what you're feeling, this practice, this time on your mat—or with your journal—has the opportunity to become deeply healing.

Very often, the biggest obstacle to our awakening, healing, and transformation doesn't exist outside of us; it exists inside of us. Letting yourself get honest physically and emotionally; not under-doing or overdoing anything at all. Just honouring the truth of your body and your heart, exactly as they are today.

Reflection
Yoga is so much more than physical. Life is so much more than physical. It's a practice of deepening the relationship you have with yourself and the world around you. It can be hard work to look at inner dialogue that is limiting or negative, but in my experience, it's the most powerful reflection you can undertake.

True Colours
Honour what you are feeling today with an honest and open heart.

Shining

Intention
Do you ever take a moment to acknowledge all the ways that you shine? Do that now with a few slow breaths. Acknowledge this as truth and celebrate it. When others light up when they see you, it's because you shine. When you make someone laugh to tears or when you validate a person who was feeling invisible, it's your light that is at work. Your light making others feel safe to be themselves. Sometimes in all that you give and all that you offer, you need to pause in acknowledgment, in celebration, and in gratitude for how brightly you shine!

Reflection
You shine! Your light makes a difference! It has an impact. It creates a ripple effect of heart-centred energy, of peace and joy. Take up space with your beautiful and powerful light!

True Colours
Acknowledge your shine! Write about the ways you spread your light.

Connecting With Stress

Intention
Take time to connect to your stress, mindfully. So often our stress can take over and sit in the seat of the decision maker of your life. Stress tries to predict the future; it tries to warn you about everything that could go wrong. It does this as a false sense of protection; if I've warned you about what could go wrong, it won't be as hard to deal with when it inevitably does go wrong.

Stress lies to us, and if we aren't conscious of this, we can lose our sense of autonomy to stress. Notice when stress is present. Remind yourself that almost everything you have worried would happen never has. Quiet, stillness, and time are the antidote to stress.

Quiet calms the chatter, stillness allows space for your heart to speak, and time for quiet and stillness replenish you fully.

Reflection
Every day brings forward a choice. Practice stress or practice peace. Prioritize peace with periods of quiet, stillness, and calm, so that the voice of stress never becomes louder than the voice of your heart.

True Colours
What stress is present for you now? What lies does it tell you? What were you most recently worried about, that never actually happened? How will you let stress go?

Yin and Yang

Intention

Yin and Yang energy are opposite but interconnected forces that together create balance. In Chinese philosophical traditions the origin of Yin/Yang, Yin represents darkness and Yang light. Daylight was a time for work, play, and movement; when darkness arrived, it was time for rest. This philosophy invites us to reconnect to nature, to remind ourselves we, too, are nature.

Neither Yin or Yang is superior, and this is why the symbol representing Yin/Yang has some Yin contained within the Yang and vice versa. When embodied Yin/Yang is the process of harmonizing, inviting a dynamic balance to all things—our lives, especially.

Reflection

Answer the call of your centre for a more harmonized, balanced life. When you do this, you create more harmony in the world. Slowing down, inviting and cultivating Yin energy in our very Yang lives isn't selfish; it's critical.

True Colours

Create two columns— Activity and Peace. Brainstorm all the ways you spend time, aligning them with each column. Do this without judgement, but to bring awareness to where more balance is needed. Why? Because balance matters, and so do you.

Finding Reassurance Within

Intention
As human beings, we sometimes live from a place, or moments, of inadequacy or insecurity. Knowing we all experience this, why would we feed it by looking outside of ourselves for reassurance that we are enough? Knowing you are enough is an inside job. Take a few breaths tune into where you are needing reassurance and offer that to yourself.

Reflection
Turn your attention inward. Comfort, reassure, and uplift yourself. Remind yourself of your adequacy, your sufficiency. Practice witnessing your feelings and insecurities so that you can offer guidance and reassurance, within.

True Colours
Where do you look for validation? Knowing *everyone* faces the challenge of seeking validation from the outside rather than from within, how can you validate yourself?

Accepting Your Flaws

Intention
Two things can be true at once. Being human means we are flawed *and* we are perfect. Can you accept your flaws and let go of the relentless internal dialogue that tells you there is fixing to be done? Can you integrate and accept your flaws or imperfections? Not feeling like you have to do anything about them?

If you have a scar on your body, you've accepted it. Some might consider it a flaw. The truth is, it's not good or bad; it's part of you. Your flaws are asking to be accepted and loved. Reassure yourself of your enough-ness, exactly as you are. Reassure yourself that your flaws make you unique.

Reflection
Say to yourself, "I am human. I am perfect *and* I am flawed. By perfect design, I come with flaws that some perceive as imperfection. I will view my flaws as part of my unique perfection, and I will no longer be at war with myself."

True Colours
What flaws do you acknowledge about yourself that you are tired of battling? What flaws do you commit to accepting as uniquely perfect, making you unique?

We Are Nature

Intention
We are nature. The Earth is our body. The water, air, and fire are our body, our spirit, our aliveness. There is no separation. With this deep knowing, we hold the wisdom that the old is falling away and a new era is opening up. We can feel it.

We are being invited to trust that because what wasn't working is falling away, it doesn't mean suffering will envelop us. It means possibility now has space for our wildest dreams to become reality. All you have to do is trust and allow excitement for what's next to fill your heart and to pour out into the hearts of others. Because we are so deeply connected in nature, as nature, our excitement will be fuel for good things.

Reflection
We are nature. There is no separation. With this, our excitement for a healed and joyful world is fuel for a new reality. Trust that the best is yet to come.

True Colours
What are you excited about in the new era of humanity? Dream and believe in big and exciting things!

From Activity to Recovery

Intention
Move from the activity of the day to the recovery from the day. This doesn't mean anything negative or assuming your day was negative. We need to normalize the phase of recovery in every day. Recovery can be different for everyone; perhaps it's through movement and free expression of your body, liberating yourself from activity prescribed by work. Or perhaps it's stillness and reflection, the embodiment of peace.
Whatever it is for you, create an intention for your recovery. Fulfill that intention with love and commitment to your tomorrow-self.

Reflection
When you embrace a commitment to recovery and restoration from the day, it becomes an undercurrent of your psyche. It becomes an anchor in tranquility. Like all things we embrace and commit to, this practice becomes stronger and more automated over time.

True Colours
How do you recover from the day? How would you like to recover from the day? Perhaps they are the same; perhaps there's opportunity.

Consistency

Intention

What is your relationship with consistency? Of nourishing yourself with the power of consistency? Where have you proven to yourself that consistency is key to change, to growth, to new opportunities, to shedding old patterns and ideas?

Sometimes this means making yourself commit to the thing you don't want to do. But that part of you wants the very best for you, knows it's not up for debate. Consistency is the key to change.

Reflection

Consistent practices that support our personal evolution are rooted in self-love. On the days you'd like to abandon consistency, tune into the voice of your highest self, the part of you that wants the best for you, always. This voice will support you in staying the course of consistency.

True Colours

What has been your experience with consistency? What do you struggle with that you'd like to create a consistent commitment to? Honour this.

Trust in the Universe

Intention

Trust in the organizing power of the universe. To create organization, sometimes we have to empty all the cupboards out, take stock, and put things back in a more useful and meaningful way. Consider that this is the process happening today. It feels unsettling; so many parts of the world are in disarray. Perhaps so many parts of your life feel as though they are in disarray.

The universe can be trusted. The ego doesn't need to control everything, despite what it is telling you. Think about how good it will feel when everything is in its most optimal alignment. Then, let go.

Reflection
We live in an entangled space between the old and the new. This is why striving relentlessly for a mindful way of living, of being, is so important. It will allow us to be here. Not there, or there, but here. Now. The present.

True Colours
What does this analogy feel like to you? Can you recall a time in your life where there was necessary chaos in order for peace to be realized?

Zoom out

Intention
Where in your life do you need to find some lightness, to let go a little, to remind yourself that this too, shall pass. Often times when we are in the mud, we forget what it feels like to be unstuck. Let yourself zoom out, zoom all the way out and you'll become more clear on what matters, what doesn't and where you can bring a deeper sense of trust that this too, shall pass.

Reflection
You have gotten to the other side of every challenge you have ever faced. Love yourself gently through the new challenges with this truth in mind.

True Colours
What are you moving through right now? Imagine zooming out, way out. What does this new perspective tell you?

Seeing Yourself in Others

Intention
Can you recognize yourself in others? When someone cuts you off, is unkind or rude, do you slip into judgement? Or can you take a breath and imagine why they might be expressing themselves in that way? A way that does not align with the "good person" values of society. Pause. Do can you see yourself in them? Recall your imperfection, your bad days, or when you are overtired or "hangry" and you react in a way that's outside of yourself. Do this to calm your nervous system, to strengthen your empathy muscle, and to detach from the contagiousness of negative energy.

Reflection
Let negative energy stop with you. Not adding to it or fuelling it or propelling it forward and outward. We have all had bad days, unkind moments, moments we wish we could take back. See yourself in others. We are connected, we are human.

True Colours
When was the last time you projected judgement onto someone for their unfavourable behaviour? Looking at it now, can you lend the experience, the "culprit" some empathy? If so, how does it feel?

Judgement

Intention
Do you ever notice that when you go through periods of judgement of others, it is usually the same period that you are feeling a lower vibration and judgment of yourself? Coming from your heart and not your head will allow you to notice this and shift your energy to more self-love and compassion. Experiencing a loving world always begins with loving yourself.

Reflection
When we love ourselves, truly love ourselves, it is easier to love and be kind to others. This is why loving yourself must become your most important exercise, especially if the concept of loving yourself seems strange or abstract. Let go of self-judgement and criticism. Love yourself fully in this exact moment of you. We see the world as we are.

True Colours
Where have you been judgemental or hard on yourself recently? Can you write about this and begin to offer support and love to yourself? End this journal entry with "I love you," then underline it twice.

Sensitivity

Intention
In times when the energy around you is hyper, heightened, or chaotic, can you discern when it's not yours? Or do you absorb it, embody it?

As sensitive people, we can acknowledge painful, difficult energy and the experience of others, and take care of ourselves by acknowledging that it's not ours. When you are among people hurting, suffering for whatever reason, do you take a moment alone as your own? If so, send love and compassion to those who are suffering and return to your own sense of inner peace.

Reflection
As energetic beings, the best thing we can do to help the world and those around us is to remain grounded in our own sense of inner peace and harmony. To reset it quickly and return to it if we are swayed by any painful energy we are exposed to. The ripple effect of your grounded sense of peace will be of great importance every time.

True Colours
When was the last time you noticed that you were absorbing the energy from people who were in experiences that weren't yours? Take some time to explore that and release it.

From Caterpillar to Butterfly

Intention
The world is in a chrysalis of accelerated change; it's deeply uncomfortable, even painful at times. A period where we can experience moments of helplessness. Coming to your yoga mat, your journal, spending time in nature, or time with those you love, transforming stress, moving your body, connecting in community, are the most powerful ways you can combat the feeling of helplessness.

Preserve, protect and nurture your health, including your mental health, with all the love and compassion you so deserve.

Reflection
On days when it feels like being human is so hard, that there's so much challenge in the world, imagine the transformation from caterpillar to butterfly: the painful, restrictive process that results in

growth, expansion, and beauty beyond the caterpillar's imagination. Yes, let's imagine caterpillars, too, have the ability to imagine. All change starts with imagining what's possible!

True Colours
Reflect on a painful, challenging period in your life where, in hindsight, you realize you grew beyond anything you imagined.

Be Here Now

Intention
You are here. So, be here. Do one thing at a time, take moments of pause, moments of conscious breaths. Thinking about how busy we are and how much there is to do convinces the nervous system that things are not okay or that we are in crisis. Times might be overwhelming, but we don't have to be overwhelmed. You are more powerful than you have led yourself to believe.

Reflection
I am here. That's what is true.
I am there. This is not true.
Be in your truth. Be here now. Here is what is real; don't let it pass you by.

True Colours
Think about a time, maybe something you're moving through now, that is/was overwhelming. Can you consider that you could have moved through it with less overwhelming energy, just by being present? Write freely.

Invite Play!

Intention
When was the last time your inner child came out to play? Perhaps that part of you that deeply craved to be expressive and free never got the chance. Let yourself be silly, be playful, imaginative, and creative. In this space, don't take things too seriously; let the expansiveness of your child-like heart be explored and celebrated.

Reflection
Let your inner child come out to play. Turn up the music, dance ecstatically. Make a mess and laugh about it. Jump in a puddle, close your umbrella. Tell a joke. Laugh. Get on the ground and move freely. Age does not mean that parts of us aren't still very much alive, just waiting for you to give them permission to play.

True Colours
When was the last time your inner child came out to play? Once you've reflected on this, perhaps make space for some of that time right now. Freely.

Surrendering Control of the Future

Intention
The more you let go of trying to control the outcome, the more incredible the outcome becomes. Just by living in each and every moment with a sense of surrendering to each experience, showing up as the best version of yourself, and trusting the outcome, you will always enjoy the results.

Reflection
Our energy in every moment manifests our future. The words you chose, the integrity you display, the compassion you offer, the good will you give in your community, are all ingredients in creating a beautiful future.

True Colours
What ingredients did you add to the recipe of your future today? What ingredients can you add tomorrow?

Prioritizing Joy

Intention
What if joy and fun were the priority of humanity? What if we could flip a switch in the midst of all humans and create accountability, impose the task of creating fun and joy in the world in a giving and receiving exchange? The lightness, the ease, the peace, and love that would flow!

The truth is, each of us already has that switch, and we are the controller of turning it on and off.

Reflection
Change happens with each of us. The world will not change externally first; the world will change when individual souls put their time and energy into creating and embodying a more beautiful, joyful, fun, kind and loving space.

True Colours
Let your imagination go wild! What would it look like if the switch was flipped and creating fun, love, and joy in the world was everyone's priority?

Healing Reflection 3: Peace in Place of Pain

Invite a physical softening of your body all the way from the top of your head to the tips of your toes. Remind yourself that you are safe and that you are held and you are loved.

You've experienced so much.

So much beauty.

So much love.

And ... so much confusion.

Confusion emerged when things that were supposed to go right went wrong.

When people who were supposed to love you, hurt you.

When people who were supposed to keep you safe, scared you.

When people you gave your trust to, betrayed you.

Confusion when love became grief.

When health became illness.

When peace became chaos.

When you had plans... but life had another plan.

The lessons life, creator, universe, our souls have for us to learn, come in many ways. And many of them are wrapped in confusion.

Tonight let the true message become clear. What didn't work out, wasn't supposed to. People who hurt you or betrayed you are coming from their own unhealed wounds.

It was never about you, not being lovable.

You are on a journey. We are all on a journey. And you are not alone.

Your wounds are my wounds and my wounds are yours.

This is why we heal. We heal our pain to heal the pain around us. To end the cycles of unhealed pain. Your bravery tonight, your vulnerability tonight, your honouring of all the sacred parts within you; the sadness, the anger, the grief, are shifting the pain of the collective.

When you heal, the pain of our ancestors heals. The pain of our mothers and fathers. The pain of our children and the worlds children is being healed, when you heal. And through YOUR healing, your light will shine even brighter than it already does.

You will feel spaciousness emerge through this journey. Spaciousness you'll get to know and explore. To fill with love, hope and peace. To fill every pocket of the vastness you've allowed for and invited into your heart.

Love for yourself, love for your journey, for your life.

Hope for tomorrow and hope for what's possible in realizing your dreams. Peace in place of pain. Peace to allow acceptance for what is, for what was and peace to propel your beautiful dreams forward.

You are worthy of this place of love, hope and peace.

I am worthy of this place of love, hope and peace.

We are worthy of this place of love, hope and peace.

Because we are one.

Say these words out loud as a claiming of your truth:

I deserve to heal.

I am worthy of healthy love.

My journey is my offering.

I am loved.

I am love.

And so it is.

Wisdom From Around the World

Intention

We accept so much from around the globe. Food, music, technology. We accept these things with ease, without even thinking about it; sadly, without even acknowledging their origins.

Why, then, do we hesitate in being open to wisdom offered from around the world? We resist wisdom because of fear or threat of unknown transformation. Perhaps we resist wisdom out of something worse: ignorance. Deny ancient, cultivated wisdom from around the world and we deny ourselves the vastness and the spice of life. There is wisdom to be shared and absorbed that will nourish us and expand us beyond measure as a human species.

Reflection
Let go of any fear or potential ignorance about absorbing new wisdom from around the world. We don't know what we don't know. There are spiritual offerings and insights that can help us, grow us. Humanity is in need of all the wisdom it can get for this collective healing and expansion journey to succeed. Invite all the nourishment available. Get curious, read, listen and notice your expansion.

True Colours
What can you get curious about? What can you study about parts of the world that can offer you growth and education? What can you lean into with intention that will expand your heart and soul?

Intention of Alignment

Intention
In our practice of yoga, we often refer to alignment. We seek it in our poses, through our bodies. Today, let's cultivate a more sizable invitation to alignment. Being aligned in all aspects of our life, to what we know is good for us, to be conscious of what behaviours align to our value system. Let's align our thoughts, our actions, what we consume nutritionally, environmentally, and emotionally to our truest, most authentic self. Practice this on your mat and in your life, and notice what shifts.

Reflection
Bring a sense of alignment with you into every day. Be aware of the alignment of your values in your relationship with yourself and with others. Tiny moments of consciousness throughout the day

where you ask yourself, *Is this in alignment with my truest, highest self?* By simply becoming aware of this, by inquiring within, you'll make shifts. From there the ease of life will get louder and your energy will flow with less disruption.

Let these words land as your own: "I am worthy of full and complete alignment to my values, to my highest self."

True Colours
What parts of today were aligned to your higher self? What parts were out of alignment? Explore this honestly, without judgement. We can't shift what we don't first bring awareness to.

Seeking Truth From Within

Intention
Every truth makes us relax and every lie makes us tense. The body knows, the heart knows what is right for us, what is best for us. Sometimes we move so quickly through life, we forget to ask for guidance from within. Our intuition, our heart centre, our own inner wisdom. Like all muscles, if we don't use them, they become weak. Pause, tune in, ask within, and trust the rest.

Reflection
Notice when your body speaks to you and tune into what it's trying to tell you. Turn up the volume of your authentic voice. Your inner wisdom, your inner guru. When you feel lost or stuck, shift the energy to inquiry. You have the answers, the knowledge, and the voice of guidance within.

True Colours
Do you trust your gut? Physical moments of tenseness or ease, guiding you to what is best for you? Write about what this looks like in your life now and what you'd like for it to look like in the future.

Tune in to Your Yearnings

Intention
If your fear conflicts with what you long for, choose to let go of the fear. Fear keeps us playing small. The voice of fear comes from programing, or old experiences. So much of what we have feared in our lives has never happened. Yet we continue to let fear guide us. Tune in to your yearning, your longing, your true desires, the things that would cause you regret if you didn't at least try.

Reflection
Reflect on what you yearn for. Sit quietly, create time and space for this conversation with your soul. Feel without judgement or limitations. Put all of your fear aside and see what comes up to the surface of your heart.

True Colours
Write without thinking. What are you longing and yearning for in your life? How is fear preventing you from realizing what you are longing for?

Vitality

Intention
The presence of life energy. The bridge to this force, to what you are capable of, is found through your breath. Work with what is there today, accept what is today, as it is today. Let yourself get curious about what is possible as you explore your vitality; your body, your heartbeat, your breath. Commit to curiosity, to truly seeking the energy of vitality.

Reflection

The things I feed become stronger; the things I neglect become weaker. Your vitality is the presence of life energy. It can be explored widely, or it can be quieted and minimized. Let the waves of your breath be waves of cleansing, of preparation to make room for the exploration of this incredible life force that is you.

True Colours
When did you feel the most vitality in your life, so far? How can you invite a sense of of vitality into every day?

Letting Go of Limiting Beliefs

Intention
The thing that holds us back, puts limits on us, doesn't exist outside of us—it exists inside of us. Our own fear and limiting beliefs keep us in the same thought patterns, which turn into deep, internal programming. Maybe if we awaken our vigor, our ability to get excited about what's possible, we can expand our hearts, our vibration, and these limits will dissolve. Reprogramming ourselves to live this life fully into the realm of possibility is an inside job, one you are so capable and worthy of fulfilling.

Reflection
Imagine the life you truly desire: the goals, the dreams, the opportunities. Then remind yourself that anything is possible, because you're here.

True Colours
Take time to explore your limiting beliefs. Write about that voice that surfaces the moment you think about a big desire or dream, telling you it's not possible. Replace that voice with one that uses language to support your dreams and that reminds you to live life fully and to let go of limiting beliefs.

Sinead Moylet

Indigenous Peoples' Day

Intention
Part of our collective journey is rooted in education. Education is the antidote to ignorance. What will you do today to learn about the people Indigenous to where you live? What will you do to amplify the stories and wisdom of Indigenous Peoples?

Reflection
Education is the antidote to ignorance. It is the entryway to authentic connection. Learn something today, learn many things, seek out wisdom from people Indigenous to the land you live on and join in celebrating and honouring Indigenous Peoples not just today, but EVERY day.

True Colours
Where can you donate, spend money or time, in support of Indigenous owned businesses or non-profits? Acknowledge something you learned in your research today and share it with another.

Sending Love

Intention
Think about something or someone that fills your heart, that makes you feel the energy of devotion, that cradles you in peacefulness and that reminds you of the most beautiful expression of love. Notice how this acknowledgement floods throughout your body.

Reflection
Think of a place, a person, or a group of people that could use some of the good energy that has flooded through you today from the intention you set. Take a moment to dedicate some of this energy,

to send it to this person, place, or group of people that are struggling or suffering. Whatever way you can express that from your heart, take a moment to do that now.

You are an energetic force; the love, thoughts, devotions, intentions, and energy you send to those who need it is always received.

True Colours

In a written meditation, reflect upon the person, place, or group that you sent love to today. Write freely.

Disruption of Energy

Intention
There is a deeper understanding today about the concept of triggers or energy disruptors. A disruption in your energy that you notice right away is pointing you in the direction of your healing work. The moment we acknowledge a disruption as a tool to learn from and heal through is the moment we take our power back.

Reflection
Trust the triggers, the disruptions, as teachers. Ask yourself questions like, *Why did it sting when they said that?* will bring you closer to resolving and healing. The more often we attach to the opportunity within a trigger, rather than the trigger itself, rather than the suffering on repeat, the lighter we will become. All this to make space in your heart and your consciousness for a more joyfully-lived life.

True Colours
What are the triggers in your heart guiding you to see, to heal?As you write and feelings emerge, remind yourself that you are loved, and you are held.

The Power of Quiet

Intention
The power found within the quiet. This is where we rediscover the preciousness of everything. The pauses, the gaps, the gems only found in stillness.
We are witnessing a time of needed unravelling. All that is broken is coming to surface. A time where we need to place deep trust in the bigger, divine plan. To find that trust when we are in doubt, we need to seek and embrace moments of stillness. Quieting all the noise. Protecting our energy, spending time with it so we can contribute to a more peaceful and sound future.

Reflection
In the days ahead, consider committing to fifteen intentional minutes to sit and just be in the power of quiet. Inner stillness. A sanctuary to which you can retreat and find serenity. Maybe even discover a deeper connection to trust of the greater plan, and to your beautiful heart.

True Colours
When you sat in fifteen minutes of silence and stillness, how did you feel? Explore this thoroughly; allow for moments of realization.

Community 2

Intention
The beautiful, supportive, inclusive, and fulfilling sense of community! The system we live within might not be working, but community is, and always has. As humans, we fundamentally care about one another and want everyone to do well and be well. That's

community. Within your life, there is community – and that's worth connecting with and celebrating!

Reflection
Never let the noise of the world deafen you from what is loud and clear and worth constant uplifting and celebrating: community! It's found in smiles, in doors held open; it's found in big and small gestures, and it is all rooted in the beautiful foundation of true human connection.

True Colours
Where have you felt or witnessed community in your life? Where can you contribute to community in your life?

The Intention for Ease

Intention
We have forty-three facial muscles and six hundred muscles throughout the entire body. Take a few moments to relax and let all of them rest. The tiny muscles around your eyes, the muscle in between your eyebrows, your cheeks, your forehead, your ears, your nose, your lips, your jaw.

Continue this release, this letting go, this deflation of holding, of tension through the entire landscape of your body. Let this time be a retreat from life.

Support this time with smooth waves of breath and let your mind and your heart be in celebration of the ease you've created.

Reflection
Consider that ease is a choice. Choose to cultivate ease in your practice, in your life at work and at home. Strengthen the concept of ease, your ability to access it on demand. Do this so that it becomes

the first option when you're presented with challenge in life. Ease will bring you clarity and peace.

True Colours
What did you create when you mindfully let go of all the muscles in your body and let them rest? How did it feel? Write about how letting go can be a strength and how you've explored or plan to explore this in your life.

Love From the Inside Out

Intention
Living from the inside out. Love: not the "fluffy stuff"—which can be gold at times—but the truest state of love. Inviting love to be infused in all of the ways we operate and how we show up in the world as human beings. Love is the highest energetic vibration and, when truly embodied, attracts the same energy in return.

Love is the key to healing ourselves, our planet, and one another. It's the key to releasing suffering and living from the inside out.

Reflection
Love is the most powerful and highest of vibrations, yet so simple to embody. When mindfulness accompanies love, love guides you. One moment at a time, as you walk through life, can you tune into and allow your energy to align with love? Every word, thought, decision, every action and reaction: let love lead it all. Try this and notice the peace within that spills out around you.

True Colours
When has love guided you in a moment where you had to choose it, with effort? What was the outcome? How can love be at the foundation of all things in what you are experiencing or moving through this week?

Yoga

Intention

Our yoga mat is like a training and practice ground for life. We experience discomfort when we try new things; sometimes we lose balance and we fall. On your mat, you get the opportunity to practice responding in a way that supports deeper self-love, so that you can take this practice with you into life.

When things get seriously challenging, we can drop into our breath so the challenge doesn't dominate the experience in a negative way. Realize your power to persevere when conscious breath is present.

Practice who you want to be in life. When you fall, do it with the spirit of a child, smiling, maybe laughing and trying again and again. Allowing the trying to be part of the joy of growth. If there's discomfort, practicing bringing supportive and reassuring words, even compassion, to your mind. Let your mat hold space for you to try new things, physically, emotionally and spiritually.

Reflection

Because you show up on your mat, you are showing up for yourself; just like you are showing up for yourself in life. Acknowledge yourself for the yoga you practice here and the yoga you take with you.

True Colours

To the non-yogis: has this inspired you to try yoga? All you need is your body, a mat or a towel, and water. There are many ways to practice life in contained spaces. Look for those.

If you are a student of yoga, what have you learned on your mat? Write freely.

Make Your Mind Your Friend

Intention

Buddha said, "Your mind can be your best friend or your worst enemy." We are a result of what we have thought. Have you noticed when we have too much time on our hands the mind gets busy, noisy, even combative?

The most challenging practice for the mind are the slower times when there's space that is so easy to fill with the mind's chatter. Be one step ahead of your thoughts. Notice them, try not to attach to them all as truth. Let them float by like clouds. It takes persistent practice. But it is possible, because you are living a life of possibility.

Reflection

Your mind can be your best friend or your enemy. Notice what role it plays in every thought. Let the voice of your inner critic, your inner enemy, fade away, because you choose to pay it no attention. Attach to the thoughts that are supportive, kind, and loving. These are the thoughts born from your centre, your essence, your highest self.

True Colours

What did your inner critic say to you today that you refused to attach to? What did your inner best friend say to you that you fed with love and truth? How did it feel?

Black Lives Matter

Intention

Dr. King said, "Peace is the presence of justice. A peace where my brothers and sisters have a place and a voice at the table of humanity." Source: 1964 book "A Martin Luther King Treasury"

True peace, desiring true peace, will be evident in action. It will be evident in the education we seek and absorb; it will be evident in speaking up and speaking out. It will be evident in the voices we uplift and amplify. The work of true active allies, accomplices, and anti-racists is the most critical ingredient, the ingredient in a true end to racism. Reflect today as to the steps you are taking, have taken, or will take to contribute to a world without racism.

Reflection

True peace will be evident on the change you embody and amplify. It will be evident in the education you seek, the conversations, advocacy, friendships and in love.

True Colours

Where are you in your anti-racist education journey? What can you do today to infuse your heart and your consciousness with more knowledge?

Permission for Stillness

Intention
Creating space for stillness isn't a luxury, it's a necessity. It isn't always easy for an overloaded or busy mind to relax. Those are the minds of many, perhaps most of us in these times. We need to exercise the practice of stillness like any skill we wish to improve.

Today, give yourself full permission for stillness, for calm to wash over you. Do that now, with the invitation of your breath. Let your face be free of tension; allow your eyes to rest and restore in their sockets. All the muscles you've used in your body today, let them rest for a few moments here. Letting go of holding in the body and the busy-ness of the mind, we make space for new energy to flow with ease. To attract the very things that we need and desire.

Reflection
Balancing by turning our attention from the outer world to our inner world. Deepening our awareness of our relationship to ourself. Stepping into our innermost room of consciousness and peace, where we are comfortably enveloped and wrapped in bliss. Your own personal space for presence, tranquility, and transformation.

True Colours
How is your stillness practice progressing? Can you take ten minutes in stillness now, to get clear on what that answer might be, if it's not coming to you with ease?

Remembering the Essence of Your Soul

Intention
Trusting, remembering. Coming back to the essence of your soul. Coming back to the you who you were before things happened to

you. The optimism, the joyfulness, the self that felt safe and embodied the purest love. Trust. Remember the truth of our souls' journey: that we are always exactly where we need to be. Remembering that after all the hardship, there were lessons realized and growth found. Your growth.

Remembering and reconnecting to your part in the evolution of humanity, just by taking up space as you. Creating a humanity that leads with love, gratitude, and peace.

Reflection
Remember, your soul is on a journey that it signed up for. Seeking lessons, healing, and striving for pure, loving acceptance of all things, especially the essence of who you are.

True Colours
Can you look at all you've overcome and see your growth? Write about what changes when you trust your journey.

Transformation Through Care

Intention
Every time you have an energy that needs to be transformed, like jealousy or fear, anger or sadness, do something to care for this energy. Rather than letting it hurt you, care for it. Turn and face it; look at it and ask it what it needs. Listen for the response. Let it come from your heart. In doing this, you can experience the same outcome you experience when you care for a plant, a child, a physical wound: healing.

Reflection
Tend to your more difficult energy with a peaceful approach. Remove judgement and attachment and lend your nurturing, supportive heart to its resolve.

Sinead Moylet

True Colours
Isn't it liberating to step into a practice of caring for your more challenging emotions? How have you tried this? If you haven't, imagine yourself trying it; perhaps it means looking back. You are held.

Begin again

Intention
Every day we get the opportunity to begin again. If you think about it, the greater truth is that every moment, we get the opportunity to begin again! Show up for the moments in your life with total presence. So life doesn't feel ordinary or mundane and so that you will know when it becomes that way and you can choose to begin again. Be so present that you can see quickly where there is an opportunity to shift, to re-start or regain the traction of progress and growth. New beginnings are always available to us.

Reflection
Let yourself begin again, begin again, begin again.
Allow for so many beginnings that you enjoy the journey and let go of the destination.

True Colours
Where was there an opportunity to begin again today? Did you take it? Can you imagine what tomorrow would look like if you give yourself permission to begin again?

Chosen Family

Intention
Family isn't always blood. Family is the people in your life who see you, who root for you and accept you for who you are and who you are not. Pause here and bring to your heart the people in your chosen family.

Reflection
You have collected people along the way. People who have appeared exactly when you needed them. They have taught you lessons about life and about yourself. They have shared their experiences and they've expanded your heart. Thank someone who has loved you and become your family.

True Colours
Who are the people in your chosen family? Celebrate them; send them love.

Learning to Thrive

Intention
Some of us are more aware of our healing, growth, and self-discovery journey than others, and that's okay. Life is about realizing that everyone is on their own personal journey, and sometimes journeys look very different.

We don't heal, grow, and discover ourselves on a deeper level for only ourselves. We do this so we can thrive in this life, so that humanity will have an easier, more peaceful journey. Take one day at a time, one moment at a time, and one breath at a time. You're on your way to thriving.

Reflection
While the only way out is through, don't forget that by letting go of old stories and patterns that don't propel us forward, we are making space for patterns and stories that do. We are preparing to thrive.

True Colours
Does the idea of thriving excite you? What can you let go of today to make space for yourself to step into thriving? What can you invite in today to grow your ability to thrive?

Gratitude

Intention
Gratitude gives way to the fulfillment of life. When we place intention and attention on all of the things that we are grateful for, we become aware of just how sweet life is. Perhaps the things you're grateful for were once challenges. Perhaps the things you're grateful for were, at one point, not enough. Look at all you've been blessed with and celebrate with sweeping, glowing, joyful gratitude.

Reflection
Gratitude is the key to shifting your perception of life. Why not place your attention on the countless blessings and gifts, big and little, seen and unseen, that are all around you in abundance.

True Colours
Write everything you are grateful for. Write and write and write. Clouds, sunshine, flowers, grass, cars, buses, friends, fruit, grains. Let this list be pages and pages and have fun flowing in the energy of gratitude. Afterwards, sit in quiet reflection, absorbing it all.

Taking Time to be and become

Intention
Let the events of today and yesterday fade away. Breath in deep; sigh, exhale. Do that again. One more time. Let any worry or thoughts about tomorrow quietly dissolve. Lovingly remind yourself that you deserve this time, this practice. That you deserve to slow down to balance and restore your nervous system. To recharge and reset in a deeper way.
    Be peace.

Reflection
Be the stillness, the quiet, the calm, the tranquility. Be the kindness, the inclusiveness, the acceptance, the ease. Be the reflection of love. At the root of it all, be the peace you wish to see in the world.

True Colours
What can you add to this list of being and embodiment? What else should we be so that we can see more of it in the world?

Loving Kindness

Intention
Catch your mind when it is delivering unkind messages to your heart. Replace those messages quickly with the ones you would say to someone you love. Take some time here to breathe and to become the observer of your thinking mind.

Reflection
The world isn't getting darker. It feels that way, I know. It is detoxifying and purging and within this process, the toxins must eventually become exposed. Your heart centre, your presence, your kind and

loving thoughts, your healing, your growth, are the antidotes the world needs. Keep shining, dear one.

True Colours
What unhealthy or toxic thought patterns can you bring to the surface and allow yourself to detoxifyfrom by asking them to leave your consciousness?
This may take time. Be loving, kind and patient with yourself.

Decisions

Intention
Life is a series of tiny decisions; even the big ones can be small in the grandness of your life. Decisions like in a game of chess, where small, mindful choices create outcomes a few steps afterwards. When we do this, we reduce overwhelm. We begin to influence long-term changes by making decisions that come from love.

Simplify your thought process. Before eating something, asking yourself if it is poison for your body, or medicine. Choose with the scales favouring medicine. An investment in future you. When you choose words, too, ask them if they are poison or medicine.

Choose to live and be in a way that serves the future version of you. Make tiny decisions today that will inspire more peace and ease and that will inspire those around you to do the same.

Reflection
Together we are a force that can make change in our lives and in the world, just by making tiny decisions all day long that are rooted in love.

True Colours
Look at the decisions you made today without judgement and notice where the practice of mindful decision making might have shifted some of them.

You Are Enough

Intention
Your worth is not defined by how many things you say yes to, especially when you want to say no. When you fail, it does not change your worth. This is what's true.

The stories we have created because of love that was conditional—sometimes even self-love that was conditional—are simply not true. You aren't loved for what you do, you are loved for who you are. Your essence, that part of you that arrived into his world, the part of you that will go with you when you leave. Let go of anxiety and messaging about not doing enough, or that how you've lived so far, isn't good enough. It's not about how much you get done or how much money you make. This journey is about being true to you.

Reflection
Perfectly, beautifully, you. To feel love for who you are, as you are. The most sacred gift, of self-worth and self-validation, a gift we have the opportunity to give ourselves. Perfectly, beautifully, you.

True Colours
Where do tapes play about your enough-ness? What can you say to override those messages that simply aren't true?

Listening to Your Highest Self

Intention
Drop out of your mind and into your heart where your highest-self resides. That part of you, at your core, that is free of worry and full of trust, because this is the part of you holds a deep knowing, a deep understanding of your journey. If you ask it right now, what message would this part of you have for you today? It may feel like you're making it up when the answer comes, but trust it nonetheless. Soon, this relationship will get stronger and so will your trust of this voice. The highest version of yourself that will never let you down.

Reflection
Invite conversation with your highest self. Your intuition, your always-knowing. Allow trust and a sense of safety with this part of you. Allow the self-love that comes flowing through because of it.

True Colours
Consider a daily practice of asking, "What does my higher-self want to say to me today?" Listen for the answer and write it down. Just a line or two. Again, it might feel like you're making it up; that's okay. Soon, you'll come to know that the voice responding is rooted in the wisdom of your true essence..

Polarity

Intention
There is a deep polarity in the world and it can be confusing at times. In your own life you may be feeling less attached to your past. Perhaps you're noticing that certain aspects of your past that felt heavy are feeling a little lighter, even if some aspects still feel heavy.

You are realizing that keeping track and replaying doesn't serve the evolved you that you're becoming. You might be experiencing a sense of peace.

The world around, filled with significant unrest, feels so opposite to this sense of peace. Let yourself stay focused in the face of it all. Stay the course of finding peace, healing, and letting go. The world will catch up, and it will do so more quickly the more of us that charge the battery of peace.

Reflection

You are the counterbalance to these turbulent times. The work you are doing, your beautiful, peaceful energy, your letting go of old stories and worries. Your inviting in of trust, optimism, belief, and hope is a gift. The energy of the world around you is the recipient, including your loved ones, and yourself.

True Colours

Have you noticed that you are letting old stories go? Take some time to acknowledge and reflect on the stories that used to run you that you've let go of or are in the process of letting go. Send gratitude to your heart for this work and the value it has in your life.

Honouring Rest

Intention

So often we fight, resist, or question our energy unless all is well, unless we are feeling good. Honour your tiredness, the low vibration days, without making them mean something is wrong. Together, we often acknowledge that we are energetic beings; with all that surrounds us in the world, we are bound to feel days of fatigue or even sadness that we can't put our finger on. The key is to notice it, without attaching any sense of permanence to it. Love yourself through it just like you would a loved one outside of you. Nurture yourself. Honour what is.

Reflection
On days when low energy or low vibration meets you, honour it. Honour your tiredness. Curl up, rest, renew, without question, without judgement. Do all the things for yourself that you'd do for someone you love. Anchor yourself in love for yourself.

True Colours
How have you honoured your tiredness recently? Or, how have you not honoured it, or judged it, made it mean something? Write, notice, and do it with love.

Healing Reflection 4: Hold Space for Your Heart

In this moment, you are holding space for you. Holding space for your heart. You are spending time with your feelings from experiences that changed you. Old experiences, recent experiences. Holding the parts inside of you that hurt. Honouring and allowing for emotion that has built up and accumulated to be fully felt. Spending time to feel the feelings from stress of the day to life living in a world that feels uncertain. Spending time with the traumas that rocked you. Loss that broke your heart.

You are safe. In this moment, remind yourself that you are safe. You have turned inward to hold and love yourself in this moment. You are caring for yourself the way you have needed to be cared for. Reminding your heart that because others didn't, or haven't, doesn't mean *anything* about your worthiness.

Let yourself feel wrapped in a blanket of love.

What you have moved through the confusion, the hurt, feelings of being lost, is being released as you write your True Colours, as you read, as you move, feel and cry.

You are honouring all the parts inside.

In this honouring, you are letting go of the stories attached to the experiences you lived through. Stories that kept you scared. Scared to forgive or be forgiven. Stories that told you to keep everyone else happy and that your happiness would come later. Stories that told you you're to blame.

These stories have been lies. Lies that are limiting and keep you rooted in those challenging experiences. Tell the stories you don't need them anymore. They may have emerged to try and protect you, but you are stronger now.

You don't have to outsource your validation anymore. You have the power to validate yourself, to remind yourself and the small child within you that you are *so* profoundly special. Accept your wholeness. Accept all of you, in deep reverence for the strength you have that has carried you.

It is said that enlightenment is a series of softenings.
Bravely invite ease into your heart.
Bravely release the pain, and just as bravely keep the love.
Free and uphold the true essence of you, underneath the experiences.
Let the tiny blessings, the blissful moments in this life fill you with warmth. Let the connection to your peace within uphold you in love every single day.
Let's take a few cleansing breaths together.
Inhale forgiveness.
Exhale guilt.
Inhale love.
Exhale blame.
Inhale acceptance.
Exhale worry.
Inhale peace.
Exhale sadness.
Inhale ease.
Exhale heaviness.
Inhale community.
Exhale loneliness.
Inhale the light.
Exhale the shadow.
Say out loud.
I am releasing the pain.
I am keeping the love.
I claim peace.

Ego Death

Intention
Yoga doesn't need you or want you to force yourself into a pose. The ego may want you to, though. Being on your mat is a powerful opportunity to practice noticing when the ego creeps in. Practicing this here, so that when we are out in our lives, we can do the same. Notice ego; let go of the stories and lies it tells us about what we "should" be doing. Not pushing ourselves past fatigue, past the need for water, because it tells us we will appear weak. The truth is, taking rest and water when the body asks for it is strength.

Reflection
Ego seeks to serve itself. It ignores the needs of your heart and your soul. Life is not a competition. It is a journey to your heart, where the soul speaks gently and lovingly, guiding you to challenge and compassion equally.

True Colours
How has your ego shown up lately? Write, inquire, discover.

Answers Found in Silence

Intention
So much of this practice is about removing the clutter and the chatter in the mind. Piercing through the veil of endless story-telling and narration. Quieting the mind, understanding in a deep way the universal language of silence and coming home to our centre. Accessing the silence behind the mind where the most wonderful sense of peace lives.

Sinead Moylet

Reflection
Silence is a source of great strength. It is not emptiness; it's a bountiful place of answers through contemplative meditation. It is bliss, it is peace, it is yours whenever you invite it.

True Colours
Where did you find silence today? What answers came up in the clarity of the silence you sought?

Winds of Change

Intention
Sometimes it is through the winds of change that we find our true direction. Winds that disrupt, that are erratic and unpredictable. This reminds us of life when change is present. This experience can be unsettling, because we prefer to know what is coming, what's happening, what's next. But the wind reminds us that while we never truly know, we can equip ourselves with the tools to withstand the winds. To be ready for the winds of change and all she offers.

We equip by healing, by coming to terms with difficult truths, by challenging our inner "worst case scenario" critic, and by growing in our ability to cope. The winds in nature are an offering of energetic clearing, just like the winds of change in life.

Reflection
Trust your journey over and over again. Sometimes, in the winds of change, we find our true direction. The wind reminds us that the only way we can respond to her, to disruption, to uncertainty, is by adjusting our sails. We may not have power over what is happening in our life, but we always have power over our response.

True Colours

When have you felt like something was happening that you had no control over? Did you remember your power to respond in a way that served your highest good in that moment, or was it realized later, perhaps even now?

Choose Your Healing—Relentlessly

Intention

You are on this journey of discovering your truest, brightest colours, because you know that something else is possible; that you are possible! By finally spending time with yourself, with the big emotions from life's hard experiences, you'll be able to honour them and release them. Honour the sadness, the grief, the anger, the fury, and release it all. You are allowing all the feelings you have never had the time or support to move through to be felt fully. Releasing in this way of self-discovery doesn't mean you don't honour the truth of your experiences. It means you are loving yourself hard enough to know the pain of the experience is not meant to be held onto.

Happiness is inside of you, waiting to be expanded as the walls come down. Walls you once needed but that you are ready to let crumble because you are stronger and more equipped to deal with all that life presents to you. Let your happiness flow freely without waiting for it to leave.

Reflection

Choose your healing and happiness relentlessly. Say to yourself, I am releasing the pain of my past. I am keeping the love of my past. I am healing. I am choosing happiness. I am worthy of the happiness that lives inside of me, the happiness I choose when I choose to heal.

Sinead Moylet

True Colours
Celebrate your journey; acknowledge your growth and the healing you are choosing in this very moment. Write freely.

Notice When Things Bother You

Intention
When we are bothered by something, it is coming from inside of us. The disruption we feel inside when we are sitting in heavy traffic or if the line at the supermarket is moving slowly. When we realize this, we can change it. We can make a conscious decision not to be bothered by things we have no control over. We can decide not to hurt ourselves by the experience of stress when stress isn't necessary. This is our personal power that we must exercise and celebrate. .

Reflection
When something causes the feeling of stress to arise inside of you, ask yourself if it's stress that is necessary or if you can let it go. These are the moments, the growth opportunities, that give way to a life without so much stress. The line ups, the traffic, the weather, the socks outside of the hamper—let go, let go, let go. It's only disrupting your peace, after all.

True Colours
What caused stress for you today that you now realize wasn't stressful at all?

Move With Intention

Intention
Move today to let go of stress energy that has the potential to make you feel unwell. Move to work through challenges. Move to celebrate your body, your vitality, and your life. Sweat to release worry, and frustration. Move today because you can. Move today to get to know yourself better and be witness to your strength, your resilience, your growth and perseverance.

Reflection
After the movement comes the stillness. The place behind our mind where our hearts can be heard.

True Colours
Have you moved today? If not, do that now; dance! Shake! Run or jump! Can you acknowledge the energy you moved, released, allowed?

Your Body Is A Masterpiece

Intention
The body is a masterpiece, and when we take care of it, we create and add to the longevity of life. Sometimes, we take care of others more than we take care of ourselves. We give advice for well being that we struggle to take ourselves. Continue the journey of turning love inward and refusing to be hard on yourself in the process. The harder we are on something, the faster we wear it out.

Reflection
Take care of yourself inside and out. Nurture yourself out of pure love and respect for your beautiful body, mind, heart, and soul. Love yourself harder, every day of your life.

True Colours
How did you take care of your beautiful vessel today?

Acknowledge Fear Of The Unknown

Intention
If we are eventually glad for our experiences, for the lessons they gave us, for the ways in which we grew and became better than before, why do we still let ourselves fear the unknown and suffer when things are unknown? We will never be able to predict the future. Let yourself exhale a thousand times a day. Let yourself love and enjoy every moment of this life.

Reflection
Elevate the best version of yourself, the version that isn't scared of the unknown, that allows you to trust. That version of you that lets go of what does not serve you, in every single exhale you take a thousand times over, every single day.

True Colours
What scares you about the unknown of the future? Write, acknowledge it. Take many, many breaths, letting more and more of that fear go with every exhale. We cannot change what we don't first acknowledge. Then, simply notice.

Fathers Day

Intention

The biggest gift any father can give to himself, and his children is to heal. The biggest gift any man can give to children of the world is to heal. Heal from the wounding of the world that made him fit into a box that at times, denied his humanity. That denied him the ability to feel his feelings fully and safely. Fathers Day can mean many things to many people. For some, today is painful, grief filled and confusing. For some, it is celebratory, and love filled and happy. All of you matter in this moment. And honouring your truth will pave the way for greater celebration for future generations.

Reflection

Men and Fathers who bravely heal their wounds, heal the wounds of those around them. In gratitude to all men who lead, coach, inspire, support and uplift the children in their lives.

True Colours

What does Fathers Day mean to you? Reflect on this from as many perspectives as you can.

A Life Fully Lived

Intention

A life fully lived is a life full of growth, change, and overcoming challenges. Not staying in predictable patterns but seeking experiences that challenge and change us. Experiences that we know will create a little discomfort—sometimes a great deal of discomfort.

Use your outlets, your mat, your journaling, your free dance expressions as the playground for growth.

Reflection
Change creates challenges. Challenges create discomfort and disruption. Change creates courage. Challenge creates opportunities. All of this creates a levelling-up of your heart, mind, body, and soul.

True Colours
Is there change in your life currently that you can step into with the intention of growth? Perhaps change you have avoided that you are ready to seek and step into?

Life's Situations

Intention
Some situations in life are easy to move through. Some are challenging and difficult. Some are boring or even mundane. The poses, postures, and flows on our mat are symbolic of these situations. Have the wisdom and recognition to stay rooted in your breath. In the consistency of mindful breath and in the compassion you extend to yourself, and the encouragement from within, you will realize the depth and vastness of your being.

Reflection
Every time we flow on our mat we have the opportunity to strengthen consistency, mindfulness, compassion, and endurance. These things are the doorway to making all of your dreams come true.

True Colours
Write freely. What does life look like for you right now? Where can you lend yourself these tools of consistency, mindfulness, compassion and endurance?

Trust Your Ability To Trust

Intention
How do you align with trust? What is your relationship with trust? Do you question it? Do you ask it for proof? Is it earned or is it embodied freely? Perhaps trust is a wound, perhaps trust is a lesson, maybe it's a beacon of light you are striving to get to.

What about trust within? Trust of your intuition to know what's best for you? Trust of your gifts and your talents. Trust of your journey, your life's path. What about the harder things, those moments when we feel a surge inside, an intensity, a trigger? What if you trusted your triggers as tools guiding you toward an unhealed wound that needs your love and attention?

Trust is the way. Trust your ability to trust.

Reflection
Consider that trust is a tool taking you closer to personal freedom, to believe that tomorrow will be better when today feels hard.

True Colours
What has been hard to trust lately?

Force Versus Grace

Intention
Where might you be forcing something in your life, perhaps on someone else, perhaps on yourself? What would it look like to choose grace instead? To make an invitation to what grace might have to offer? Perhaps more flow, perhaps letting go or access to ease where there is rigidness. Choose some grace in your life and in your circumstances. Be gentler with your heart and with the hearts of the loved ones around you.

Sinead Moylet

Reflection

Allow for more grace to flow through you. Release pressure and agendas and force. You have done so much work; you are ready to let grace and flow be a strong part of your journey. Add grace to your plentiful and love-filled toolkit.

True Colours

What are you forcing right now that you can extend some grace to? Perhaps in yourself or someone else? Write, reflect, extract the lessons you offer yourself through continued self-discovery.

Acquaint Yourself With Your Impatience

Intention

Where are you being impatient with life? Where are the places in your life that you tell yourself you are falling behind? Breathe. You are always right on time. We have worked to embrace uncertainty, yet we still let ourselves be impatient. Embrace patience as the antidote to worry.

Grant patience to that part of life where you feel like you're not far enough along, that you just acknowledged. Take a few breaths. Notice what patience has gifted you.

Reflection

Patience is a powerful warrior and one of the antidotes to worry. Patience is not passive; it is expansive. It is allowing and it is trusting. Patience is the secret to tenderness, to the unleashing of joy and the gateway to possibilities you never imagined.

True Colours

What's got you feeling impatient lately? Where is the impatience rooted? Write, explore, acquaint yourself with the impatience you are feeling.

The Horizon For Humanity

Intention

My hope is that we are all looking out at the same horizon for humanity. When you think about the future do you see it on the other side of all the violence and dismantling of systems? Let's look there now. Imagine a sense of community and belonging regardless of where you go. The ease of access to all things supporting human dignity and ease to live freely. See the connection to nature, the remembering that we *are* nature. See the inclusion, the acceptance, the honouring of differences, the evolution in our connectedness to one another.

Children being seen and heard and valued as the caretakers of the future that they are, because we have created the time and intention to honour them in this way. Can you let yourself dream of a future where hate has no place, where ignorance is melted away by education and truth? We can use the loving force of our energy to create a horizon that course-corrects all the ways we got it wrong. As energetic beings, we can make this horizon—and anything else you have hope for—a reality.

Reflection

Let yourself dream about the world you want to live in, the world you want to create for future generations. If enough of us look toward and embody the same horizon for humanity, it will be the most priceless investment we could ever make. Let yourself imagine this place, this world, this existence, and then let yourself smile about it.

True Colours

What else do you see on the horizon for a better world? Journal, create, discuss, inspire, liberate.

Permission to be Joyful

Intention

Say out loud: "I do not need to earn joy." I give myself full permission for joy." Take that permission and choose it by inviting a smile when you wake up in the morning. The first expression your face makes each day, sending a message of joy to your heart. Let it be an intentional practice until it feels natural.

Smile in demonstration that you are ready and open for what the day has to offer. Joy in blessings, joy in challenge. This is not toxic positivity, this a remembering of who we came here to be. Joyful, peaceful, human beings with light in our hearts. While difficult feelings will come and go, remember that you are so worthy and deserving of joy, too.

Reflection

Roll down the windows, turn up the music, marvel at nature, hug a tree, hug a human, dance, play, explore, discover. Choose your happiness every day of this life. You are so worthy.

True Colours

What did you do today and what will you do tomorrow to seek and embody joy?

Remembering The Nature That Is You

Intention
Think of the last time you enjoyed being outside freely on a beautiful day. Once you're there, recall the feeling of that day into your heart. Invite that energy into your yoga or movement practice today. The energy you felt with the sun warming you, birds celebrating life in song, even the smell of that memory, the sweetness of life in growth and change. Nature fills us up because we are nature. We are just another kind of species populating the planet. Today in your body and on your mat, let that feeling flow. Be light in your heart and loving with your breath. Let your mind rest while you move and feel. Let your body *feel* like another perfect part of nature.

Reflection
When all the twists and turns of life feel overwhelming, remember that you are an infinitely wise and perfect part of nature. Let this simple and beautiful truth hold you close today, dear one.

True Colours
Write about how it feels to be in your favourite outside place. Celebrate yourself as part of nature.

Release Complicating Thoughts

Intention
Release complicating, resisting thoughts and allow yourself to answer the invitation to an approach of peacefulness. Allow for acceptance about what simply is, reminding yourself that any discomfort is impermanent. Practice the art of being with yourself in a loving and supportive way. When we embody peace, peace aligns to the core of our being.

Sinead Moylet

Reflection
You embraced peace. That doesn't mean you weren't met with resistance or avoidance or disruption. It means you returned over and over to acceptance and ease, making your way to peace. Bring this magic with you. Bring peace with you, and acceptance that all things change.

True Colours
Where are you feeling resistance in your life? Can you support yourself in a conversation using the tools you have gathered so far? I think you can.

Validate Yourself

Intention
In looking back at my own healing journey, I can see that I had a pattern of looking outside of myself for validation. What I have learned in my journey through consciously, intentionally deepening my relationship *to* myself was that I can reassure *myself*. I can validate myself and I can lift *myself* up. When I do, life gets easier, and I feel stronger. Reflect on the ways that you can validate yourself today. Reassure yourself that you are doing enough, that you are a good human who deserves good things. Validation from the outside from those we love is beautiful, but validation from within is magic.

Reflection
Validate yourself. Lift yourself up. Believe in your incredible gifts! Shine light on yourself, a bright light. Then hold yourself, just like you do for others.

True Colours
Write. Give yourself a pep talk. You know what you need to hear today.

Silence Can Be Compassionate

Intention
In this life we all experience stress and negative emotions; they are so innately natural and human. The key is to extend compassion to yourself so that you can steer yourself toward a more motivating, positive energy. Let compassion be found in stillness. Pause the activity of life to be with yourself, with your heart, softening all the amour inside and out and letting the deeper parts of you be heard.

Access the deepest physical parts, as well as the deepest unseen pats of our heart and intuition, in a good, long deep stretch of the tissue and fascia. Let every gentle breath flow over the next, while allowing access to deep quiet. Land your heart gently in the sweetness of compassion for yourself.

Reflection
Today, you invited and accepted the energy of compassion and stabilization turned inward. Sit with gratitude of yourself, for the life you have created. There is a sweet, still, and compassionate place inside of you where you can land anytime you need it, even if the world around you remains noisy.

True Colours
Sit in compassionate silence for five minutes, then write freely. What did the silence tell you?

Believing Will Help You See

Intention
Believe in your worth, the value you add to the world around you. Believe in your journey, the good and bad. Believe that you'll always get to the other side of every challenge that you are met with. Believe that you are contributing to a more peaceful world just by being here. Believing that life can be joyful. Believing in these things is a choice, a powerful choice that will give you strength on days you need a little more.

Reflection
Believe that you will grow from all the discomfort on your path, just like you always do. Believe that ease, peace, and joy aren't for other people; they're for you.

True Colours
What else can you believe and affirm that will uphold your journey of healing and growth?

Progress, Not Perfection

Intention
Strive for progress, not perfection. Check in with yourself. How is it going? Don't be hard on yourself if you have wavered. There are two things that are key in transformation: recognizing when we waver, and simply coming back to where we want to be. Meet your awareness of wavering with love and compassion. You are a brave soul on a mission. You've got this!

Reflection
Strive for progress, not perfection. There are plenty of battles yet to be overcome; don't let battles within yourself take away your valuable time and powerful, precious energy.

True Colours
How is your year going? What is the energy you are feeling now? Remember, the inner critic isn't invited to this conversation.

Be Responsible For The Energy You Bring Into Every Space

Intention
Dr. Jill Bolte said, "Please be responsible for the energy you bring into this space." Have you ever gone home at the end of a challenging day or a day that required a lot of your energy, and you exude "don't talk to me, don't expect anything from me" energy? Or perhaps if life is a solo journey right now, and you enter spaces outside of work exuding the same energy. The grocery store, the coffee shop.

Given that you are an energetic being, your energy has a ripple effect on those around you. It might even cause hurt. Instead, *check in* with your energy *before* you enter every space. Ask what you might need and communicate. "I'm tired, I don't have much to give but I do love you." Or, "If I seem low, it's me moving through a challenging day; it's nothing you have done, I love you." This is also an exercise in self-love.

Reflection
As energetic beings, we must be responsible for the energy we bring into every space. Another tool for your toolkit, one that reminds you of your powerful heart and how much you matter.

True Colours
Reflect on this. Can you recall a time when you entered a space with heavy, frustrated energy and it affected those around you almost instantly?

Share Your Positive Energy

Intention
Because you are a powerful, energetic being, the ripple effect you have can be incredibly uplifting and motivating. When you've had a great day, a day full of accomplishments and being grounded in yourself, you come home and those who've had a not-so-great day are uplifted by you! Celebrate this, as your high vibrational energy is making such a difference in the lives around you.

Reflection
Checking your energy before you enter a space is a moment for you to honour what is true today. Do this without judgement, simply noticing and acknowledging. Let your higher-self tell you what you need in that moment before engaging with others. Perhaps that voice will say, *I know today was hard; it's not permanent. Be gentle with yourself, breathe."* Or, *I saw how present you were today and how much you got through and overcame! Don't rush by this incredible feeling; share it with those you love.*

The voice of your highest self will be known by this key identifier: it will always be kind.

True Colours
Recall a time where your vibration was high, when you entered a space and lit the room up. Celebrate yourself and your energy.

Stress Stories

Intention
There is some stress we can't control. Things happen that would cause stress to any human being, no matter the work they've done. We generate some stress ourselves, when we make stories about what happened into something that is unaligned to truth.

Mitigating the impact of whether the situation is unavoidable or not, remember: it's not what happens to you that increases your levels of stress, it's the stories you tell yourself. These stories serve only to make events, even minor ones, mean something about you or about your life that simply aren't true.

Reflection
There is nothing wrong with you at all. Your stress and anxiety is a response to an abnormal situation. Let go of shame. It does not serve the healing of your stress and it is full of untruth. The suffering you experience isn't because of you; it's not your fault. Use the tools you've collected and support your heart with love, breath, and kind words.

True Colours
Reflect upon a recent stressful situation you experienced; perhaps you are in one now. What did the voice of stress say to you? Did the voice of shame emerge? Take some time to explore this and to realize how useless it is to be unkind to yourself. End your reflection with kind, loving, supportive affirmations.

Sinead Moylet

Saying No 2

Intention
"No." Pause, then say it again: "No." Breathe. Check in. How does the word "no" feel inside of you? Often, this word rattles us. We associate it with being difficult or conflictual, even aggressive. This is programming, conditioning that told us we must please everyone to be loved. Some of us say yes when we *want* to say no, fearful, we will appear unhelpful or selfish, or worried we won't be liked. We feel we must *earn* the world's validation.

What is the impact on you when you say "yes" instead of an authentic "no" that wants to be said? Be true to you, without endless explanations. When "no" is your authentic truth, let it be said. Let it be lovingly owned. Let it be love, turned inward.

Reflection
You are enough. I'll say it again: you are enough. Check in. How do the words "You are enough" feel inside of you?

Your worth is not defined by whether you say "yes" to the point of overwhelm. "No" does not change your worth. Let go of stories that were created because of love that sometimes felt conditional, perhaps sometimes still does. Sometimes self-love is conditional, but you're changing that by letting your authentic "no" be said.

You. Are. Enough.

True Colours
When was the most recent time you said no? How did it feel? Was it met with acceptance and understanding, perhaps even compassion? Or not?\Write about the parts you own and the parts you don't in saying "no."

Remembering Our Shared Humanity

Intention
We are going through most of the same or similar experiences, just at different times. If we allow this knowing, we will realize , we are far more united than divided. Remembering our power to let go negative, divisive energy that we are relentlessly exposed to. Noticing when we absorb some of that negative, even toxic energy that is not ours. Not the energy that comes with bigger, harder emotions like sadness or grief, but negative energy that is rooted in fear and divide. Energy that sometimes seeps in without permission.

Tune in today to any energy that simply isn't needed, that isn't wanted. Allow it to release through your long, slow inhales and exhales. Release the energies you were not born with and come home to the essence of yourself tonight. The peace within, just waiting to emerge.

Reflection
We are far more united than divided. We are rooting for one another more than external forces want us to believe. Turn off the news, turn on your curiosity for all the ways we are the same, and lovingly celebrate all the ways we are different.

True Colours
What does this reflection inspire inside of your heart? Where can you learn more about human differences so that they become a gift that unites us rather than divides? Write freely.

Sinead Moylet

Pay Attention

Intention

Pay attention to the shadow energy that surfaces in hard times. Pay attention to how it tells you stories about suffering and permanency of suffering as if it's your life's quest to suffer. Pay attention to what is a "no" and what is a "yes" in your life, and honour both fully. Pay attention to light energy you've known and felt and have within, the light energy that shines brightest when you are being true to your heart.

Pay attention as the witness to all these things. As the witness, you sit in the power of choice. You can choose what you embody and what you refuse. You are in the driver's seat of your life. Take a deep breath and embody your personal power to pay attention and to choose.

Reflection

The shadow inside of us all wants to keep reminding us about how hard things are and all the bad things that did or could happen. It does this, in its own way, as a false sense of protection. You can tell this energy that you no longer need it. You can even thank it, if that feels right for you. Then say yes to lightness, to hopefulness, to trust and belief. Say yes to the truest part of you: your light.

True Colours

When you pay attention, when you place yourself in the seat of the witness, what do you notice today? Is any shadow present? Do this without judgement or criticism.

Rainy Days

Intention
Rainy days are often accompanied by a change of season, of new beginnings on the horizon. A clearing of energy, a quieting down. A beautiful excuse to get cozy, to curl up with a big mug of tea. To watch the raindrops trickle down the window with soft jazz playing, supporting their dance. To reflect and slow down. A reminder to be gentle with yourself and be tender with your beautiful heart.

Reflection
May you be wrapped in stillness and warmth as you soften into your heart for a while. May you embody the clearing, the cleansing, the nourishing of the waters as they fall. May you turn inward and see the brightness within you; the love, the quiet, the strength, the you. The truest version of you, that can be held softly by a good, rainy day.

True Colours
What do rainy days mean to you? Perhaps their meaning has changed over time.

Fiery Energy of Summer

Intention
Summer is a very fiery, high-energy season. To appreciate it fully, we must invite the balance between effort and ease, of fire and water or air. Today you're doing just that, and the stillness and meditation we will embody at the completion of our practice will deepen your appreciation and presence for the high energy of summer. Breathe. Let your breath slow down this fiery time.

Sinead Moylet

Reflection
Connecting with your body signals to the mind that it can rest. That it can quiet down the narratives, the tales and chronicles of the day. Embrace the fiery and high-energy of summer with joyfulness and playfulness in your heart. Balance with connection to your beautiful vessel and your breath, to slow it all down.

True Colours
Summer feels busy! Is it? Or is it the energy around you? Reflect, write, explore. No wrong answers.

End of Summer

Intention
At the end of a month, especially a mid-summer month, a feeling of anxiousness can slowly—or quickly—begin to surface. The summer bucket list, wanting to do so much, see people, have all the summer fun. In the midst these feelings of wanting to do and see more, be sure that you're not missing the sweetness of summer. The little things that summer gifts us with, the tiny treasures found in simply being present enough to witness them.

Reflection
Tomorrow is a new month, a new opportunity to slow it all down and be present for all the tiny treasures, all the sweetness of summer, all the sweetness of life. Look for these moments with relentless presence.

True Colours
What would or could slowing down offer you right now?

The Sweetness of Doing Nothing

Intention
You are here to live in the sweet spot of life. This is the place of true power, where you allow your soul, your higher self, to guide you and hold you. We often refer to this practice as dropping out of the head and into the heart. When we do this, things become clear. Challenges become easier to move through, with less attachment and meaning, because our soul knows that "this too, shall pass." Tune into the guidance of your soul, your intuition, your higher self—whichever term feels most authentic to you—and live from the very grounded, very sweet spot of life.

Reflection
Dolce far niente: the sweetness of doing nothing. Noticing and being present for the small things, the sweet spots of life that add up to create a life of happiness and peace. Find the sweet spot of your life. Live from that place. Love from there, too.

True Colours
Write about the sweet spot of your life. What does/would it look like? How can you live from that place more than not?

Summer and Playfulness

Intention
Have you found moments of true play this summer? Moments to let your inner child appear and take up space? Play isn't just about being silly; it's about letting go. It's about experimenting, taking risks. Play is our brains' favourite way of learning, and our hearts' favourite way of lightening the load. Play is training for the unexpected. It builds our resilience, our capacity to let go of the need

Sinead Moylet

to control. Look for ways to bring moments of delight and play to summertime and to all your days beyond.

Greet today and your practice with a playful heart.

Reflection
Play, move, express, explore; greet each day with a playful heart.

True Colours
Has your playful inner child been hiding? They are still very much alive inside of you. Ask them what they'd like to do today. See what comes up. How do you get a tissue to dance? You put a little boogie in it. There, that should get your inner child going.

Until Further Notice, Celebrate Everything

Intention
Celebrate everything and all of it. Then let that celebratory energy be fuel to fill you up. Let it be fuel to let go, faster. Celebrate everything so much that it becomes contagious. Celebrate everything so much that you don't miss a thing. Celebrate everything, so much that at the end of this journey, it all makes you smile.

Reflection
Until further notice, celebrate everything. Celebrate your hair, or no hair, your eyes, your smile, celebrate the parts of your body you've been at odds with. Celebrate your relationships, your break ups, your friendships, your kinships. Celebrate your successes, your failures, your fails, your wins. Celebrate your journey, your heart, your body, your breath. Celebrate so much, that at the end of every single day, it all makes you smile.

True Colours
What will you celebrate today? Write with pure liberation in your heart. Own the celebration you so deserve.

What's Not Wrong?

Intention
Often when we notice another human appearing down, we ask "What's wrong?" Perhaps sometimes we are the one being asked. What if we normalized a follow-up question after hearing the woes of your loved one's heart?

What if we ask, what is *not* wrong? This brings the attention of our heart to the many parts of life that are going well. Parts we often take for granted. As I've said before, this is not about toxic positivity. Sure, go back to what is feeling wrong or heavy. But take a moment to balance it all out. Where our thoughts go, energy flows, and the magic in looking at what's going right puts what's going wrong into a bit more perspective. Balance what's going wrong with acknowledgement about what's going right and notice the shift it makes in your journey.

Reflection
When something is "wrong" make time and space to honour it fully. Then, in mediation, journaling, or spoken acknowledgement, look

at all that is going right. Where your thoughts go, energy flows. Sometimes, this helps us to see the ways that what's going wrong might actually be guiding or growing our hearts.

True Colours
How does this feel to you? When you ask someone what's wrong, after they share and explore fully, after you extend empathy or compassion, would you feel good about saying, "Let's take a moment to fill our hearts with what's going right?" Is this a practice you could invite inward? Flow, write, feel. There are no wrong responses.

Feel, As If It's Already Happening

Intention
Manifestation. If this is still something you struggle with. that's okay. It can feel abstract, intangible. Let manifestation be a playful part of your journey. Part of manifestation is to feel your desires as if they have already happened.

Let's be playful here and imagine one of your desires is to travel to the coast of Italy. Close your eyes; take a big inhale as if you are standing by the sea. Exhale. Again, imagine the sky, the shore, the buildings off in the distance, the people, the smells. Take a big inhale; exhale. Imagine how you feel there, imagine the energy of freedom, of celebration that you did it! You're here! You're on the coast of Italy! You have days ahead to explore, to eat, to appreciate the culture, to practice the language. You're here. Stay there for several more breaths; let your mind be your tour guide. Pause. Allow for this time to dream, to feel. Slowly returning to now. How do you feel? This is manifestation, and this is living, too! Your mind is a powerful tool if you utilize its greatest abilities, rather than letting it run you.

You used your mind, you *felt* Italy all around you. Give yourself the gift of these embodied meditations and manifestations more often. Yes, you still need to work for the practical parts to pay for that ticket, but energetically, you are on your way. You have affirmed to your heart and soul that this is a dream you want to live out. Because of that, you will be drawn to take steps to make it happen. Close your eyes and fuel your manifestations, any time you like.

Reflection
Where our thoughts go, energy flows. This is an important ingredient in manifesting your greatest desires. Tune in to the frequency, the energy of what those dreams coming true would feel like, just like a radio. Wherever you tune in, you will receive.

True Colours
What desires and dreams are you manifesting? How can you tune in and broadcast that energy far and wide? Take some time for a written meditation; how would it *feel*? Write as if it already happened.

Your Best Interest Is At Heart

Intention
Life is too short to spend another day at odds with yourself. Let your truest expression of self love be found through releasing internal conflict and accepting all of you, as you are today. Your best interest is at heart and it will remind you that you were born to be real not to be perfect.

Reflection
As you move through the years and the vastness of your experiences try not to be at odds with yourself. And in case you need reminding today; you matter, you're loved and your presence on this earth makes a difference whether you see it or not.

True Colours
Where have you been at odds with yourself lately? Your best interest is at heart; what message does it have to offer to ease the conflict within?

The Roots of Yoga

Intention
Acknowledge, represent, respect, and honour the roots of yoga. This sacred practice is over five thousand years old, with its origins in Northern India. We have the honour and responsibility of educating ourselves about the roots of yoga and caring for the practice. Being in reverence to the history of yoga in mind and heart, every time we step onto our mats, every time we step off our mats.

Yoga is not a workout; it's a lifestyle, a practice of peace and connection to all things. When you feel that beautiful sense of healing, of self-awareness or calm centering after a practice, it is because of yoga's spiritual power. Be a voice that links these roots to your spirit, to the roots and truth of yoga.

Yoga is not about what you are doing; it is about who you are being.

Reflection
Be an active ally in the honouring of the roots of yoga. This practice is borrowed by the west, and we must take good care of it. We must not change the nature of this practice into something that is a shell of the richness and vastness of its teachings.

Yoga gives us liberation in how we move in the world. Be a voice that uplifts and amplifies the teachings, the practices, and the roots of yoga.

True Colours
Write about what yoga has brought to your life. Write a loving commitment statement about what action you will take to step into a deeper study of this ancient practice.

Special Acknowledgement: 'Embrace Yoga's Roots – Courageous Ways to Deepen Your Practice' is an excellent resource by Susanna Barkataki. Gift yourself and your practice with the history and wisdom she shares.

Tend to Your Fear of Change

Intention
Fear is resistance that makes the same journey feel like it's uphill rather than smooth, steady paving. Consider that your fear of change might be rooted in history, in past experiences. Changes that were hard or painful. Changes that were forced upon you. Where can this story be re-written? What are the history of changes that brought you the realization of your dreams? Place your heart energy there. Fear is lying to you. Love is holding you close.

Reflection
When you are in fear, you seek and accumulate false evidence. Tend to your fear of change. Get to know it and then release it. Change is constant, so why would we choose constant fear? The true self is not afraid.

True Colours
What are the changes that have brightened and expanded your life? Write, feel, liberate yourself from fear of change.

Waiting

Intention

Are you waiting? Are you waiting for your practice to begin? Consider that it already has. Just like life. We sit in the energy of waiting, when life is already happening, right now. Waiting for the job, waiting for the love, waiting for retirement, waiting for vacation, waiting for the weekend.

Waiting robs you of time. It steals the now. This moment. Be here. Let it be enough. There's nothing to wait for.

Reflection

Let go of waiting. Let go of anticipation for what comes next. The next pose, the next opportunity, the next text, the next "like." What comes next is simply another moment of now. Be in the now, let it be enough, because you are enough and that is what's true.

True Colours

What have you been waiting for that you can release? How does it feel to release the energy of anticipation, of waiting?

Letting Go of the Need to Prove Yourself

Intention

Who do you have to prove yourself to? Have you proven yourself to yourself? Invest in building the evidence that proves yourself to yourself and let the rest fall away. Invest in the dedication, discipline, love, and commitment to your goals and your dreams. For you.

Why be at risk of arriving toward the end of life's journey still replaying the lie that you're not enough? Realizing it took up so much of your energy? It is wasteful and it is a denial of truth. Spend time sitting with the evidence, the unbreakable truth, that you *are* enough. There is no one to prove yourself to, except you.

Reflection
You add to the collective. Your existence is unique, special, and sacred. You matter. You are more than enough. Let the evidence of your enough-ness be the voice you align to.

True Colours
Who have you felt you need to prove yourself to? Write, feel, release. Part What is the evidence that you are enough? Let your inner best friend write, feel, embody as truth.

Follow Your Joy

Intention
Follow the things that make your heart smile. When we bring awareness to something ordinary, it can become extraordinary. Perhaps it's something in nature; a flower with its soft petals gently fluttering in the warm summer breeze. A bird singing, communicating, just being its authentic self. Maybe it's a delicious cup of tea or a bite of freshly-baked, warm, squishy bread. Maybe it's a smile from a stranger. Look for these moments in your life, blissful moments, as if they are breadcrumbs guiding your path.

Reflection
Follow your joy. Today is a great day. I have everything I need. I have a peaceful and loving energy that allows bliss to flood through my veins. Today I will smile at a stranger, and I will let something go to make space for more joy. Today I will love myself, the greatest supporter of my joy.

Sinead Moylet

True Colours
What gives you the feeling of bliss? Write freely, let it be heartfelt, let it be true.

The Deep Medicine of Meditation

Intention
Begin to evoke the deep medicine of meditation. The medicine of quiet stillness. Of the journey, the retreat within. Let yourself be carried by the beat of your heart and the waves of your breath. Witnessing your gentle, soothing, calming inhales and exhales. Making acquaintance with the silence you have invited so lovingly. Be here, breathe here, be still. Do this now.

Reflection
Through action, through experiencing the beauty of journeying within, remind yourself how good it feels to go inside and delve into your own personal retreat, where all is always well.

True Colours
Begin with a meditation; length doesn't matter. Journey within, spend time with your breath. Then, when you emerge, write freely.

Hurt Versus Healed

Intention
Hurt people hurt people. Healed people heal people. Those times you lash out at someone with harshness that doesn't match the severity of their actions are usually the moments pointing to a place that needs healing.

When you feel an inner disruption arise like a volcano you didn't choose, pause before letting the lava flow. Breathe, look at your heart, and turn toward your inner child; ask what's needed and notice the magic that happens. This takes practice, intention, and a gentle approach to the wounds you are healing. Let the good news be that when you are in this practice, you *are* in healing. Healing that you so deserve.

Reflection
When we heal our wounds, the parts of us that needed support and love but didn't receive or have access to them, we stop the cycle of hurt people. We begin to create a new cycle of self-awareness. When these parts of us feel fully seen and are fully felt, we can become healed people, whose healing is magnified and multiplied.

True Colours
When has your volcano erupted in a way that you felt you had no control over? Let your truth flow, like the lava you felt that day, in that moment. Looking at that time now, in retrospective reflection, what was the wound saying? What did it need to feel seen and heard and supported and loved? I love you. You are working so hard on healing. Thank you.

The Molting Lobster

Intention
A lobster has a hard shell. As it begins to grow, it becomes confined, and so it must let go of that hard shell. This process is called molting.

To grow, the lobster must go through a process of painful confinement and discomfort, shedding the old shell and ultimately becoming very vulnerable as its flesh is exposed. When its new shell is found, comfort resumes in its new state of growth.

We are much the same as the lovely lobster. Growing from discomfort, through constraint and pain that sometimes we wouldn't choose, but growing nonetheless. Remember this whenever there is discomfort in life. Breathe, use the tools you have collected, and trust the molting process.

Reflection
You are always growing, changing, and evolving. Sometimes it can be an uncomfortable, even painful process. Make sure that when you find your new shell, you ease into the new version of yourself that has overcome a challenge. Celebrate your journey. Perhaps by doing this, challenge and growth will become easier; you can trust that you are simply molting.

True Colours
Reflect on a time you had to release an old shell and step into a new version of yourself. What was the vulnerability period like? What was the feeling when you realized your new shell was stronger? If you are in the vulnerable period now, know that your new shell is coming.

Letting Go of Plans

Intention
Consider the freedom of letting what is, just be. Challenge yourself to love yourself, and trust this life when things don't go exactly as you'd hoped or planned. Today, simply be at ease with what is. Let plans be written in pencil, ready to be changed to another version of what is. Make room for life. Leave room, make room, for you.

Reflection
Life is whatever we define it to be. The special occasions can be written and rewritten with a pencil, not a permanent marker. We

are the artists and creators of our lives. Be at ease with what is, look for treasures in things that appear to go wrong, by simply accepting all of our experiences as life. Through it all, make room for you to be you.

True Colours
How do you respond when plans fall through? What energy do you feel? What lessons do you learn and where is freedom found?

Winter Solstice

Intention
Winter solstice: the shortest day of the year, the least amount of sunlight. This day honours the symbolism of fire and light. The things we appreciate more when they're gone. Perhaps it points us to the opportunity to be mindful of other people and blessings in life that we may take for granted. Let solstice be a reminder to live each day with a mindset of awareness of all the gifts wrapped in people, blessings, and experiences we love. To right any wrongs and to honour their light as sacredly as we honour the light on winter solstice. Lessons imbedded in nature are gifts to the soul.

Reflection
Winter solstice, a reminder to be grateful for the light and not to take it for granted. A reminder that can be echoed in our relationships. Not to take our loved ones for granted and all the beautiful and loving light they shine on us.

True Colours
Who have you been taking for granted? This is not an invitation to be hard on yourself. Send them a love note, then write one to yourself as well. Often, we take ourselves for granted too.

Sinead Moylet

Find Your Inner Peace

Intention
When we feel depressed, we are living in the past. When we feel anxious, we are living in the future. When you are at peace, you are living in the present moment. If the present moment is one that is painful or uncomfortable, let yourself sit in stillness with your breath to dig deeper within. To a place found in connection to your breath, the gateway to feeling at peace. Pause. Keep pausing. Breathe. Keep breathing.

Continue in this way, going deeper and deeper into your consciousness of breath that takes you to this beautiful room inside called inner peace. This room that exists here and now, the only time and space that is real. This is the place of peace you can come to anytime you need it.

You are loved.

Reflection
Peace is its own reward, like a blanket of love wrapped gently around you, radiating out into the world. A world that needs your peace, that is grateful for your peace, that grows and heals because of your contribution to peace.

True Colours
How often do you visit that peaceful place within you? What does this place look and feel like? Write with ease.

Heart Opening At The Holidays

Intention
The holidays are not as much about opening presents as opening our hearts. By being in this heart-opening practice of yoga, you are acknowledging your ability to create and magnify love in the world, a gift unmatched by anything wrapped. Let gratitude for all things be on your mind and in your heart today.

Reflection
The true spirit of the holidays lives in your heart. It is the fondness for the past, the acceptance for the present, and the dreams of the future. The energy you are creating and caring for by being in this self-discovery and growth journey to expressing your truest colours is making a difference in the world.

True Colours
Reflect and write about the holiday season, whatever the holidays are or are not to you. Whatever holiday you celebrate, whatever the traditions, just be true to your beautiful heart.

Expectations

Intention
Expectations are a strong belief that something will or should happen. A belief that someone will or should achieve or do some-thing. Consider the antidote to this is clear communication: not hoping someone *knows* what you need, but loving yourself enough to *ask* for what you need.

Where in your life do you need to communicate your needs? Where do you need to let go of expectations and let be, let be, let be?

Reflection

Love yourself enough to ask for what you want and what you need in the world and from your relationships. Loving yourself is the antidote to future resentments.

True Colours

Where have you felt resentment in your life? What can you ask for so future expectations are lovingly heard? Or where can you release expectations altogether? Write. Explore. Love yourself.

Diversity. Equity. Inclusion.

Intention

Diversity: A dimensional variety, a range of human differences

Equity: Providing people with what they need to be successful and the response to support that may be unequal.

Inclusion: The environment and climate of the space is one that values all.

To go on this journey of finding and brightening your True Colours, we must step deeper into the education of diversity, equity, and inclusion that is available all around us. To look at our own judgements and biases. Our work is to change the now so that the future can be brighter for all. We can't change what we don't understand. Equip yourself with the bounty of education surrounding you. Do this, because you and your ability to make a difference matters.

Reflection

If we keep doing what we've always done, we will always get what we've always got. Be the visionary for the future and equip yourself with the lens of education. We must live in action to create the new.

True Colours
Research revolutionary activists and advocates. Inspire yourself. Documentaries, books, courses; being in the active work of change. You are a powerful change-maker!

The Power of Choice

Intention
We have so many opportunities for choice to guide the energy of our lives. We can choose to find ease in the dis-ease or to find comfort in situations that cause discomfort. We can choose to respond to challenging people with non-attachment, because we choose to believe that they know no better or that they are leading with their wounds. We can choose to listen to the voice of our intuition rather than the busy mind, full of stories. When we choose to listen to intuition we strengthen our sense of inner knowing, our inner teacher, every time.

We can choose to believe the universe is out to get us when things appear to go wrong, or we can choose to believe that the universe is conspiring for our best interest. All these choices are either rooted in fear or love. We need to bring awareness to the roots of our choices.

Reflection
The power of choice is open to you, in every moment of every day. Choose from love and notice how much more peace flows within you.

True Colours
What have you realized about your power to choose? Where do you use this power? Where can you exercise more loving choices?

To Let Go, We Must Feel

Intention
Letting go doesn't come without feeling. So often, we are told to "let go." Perhaps just as often, we speak it. I know "let go" is peppered throughout this book. But what does it mean? It can sound unintentionally flippant at times.

To let go, we must feel. We must spend time with the experience and feelings we are wanting to let go of and wanting to fully release. If there's something you need to let go of, spend time with it. Feel the emotions that need to be expressed and honoured and moved through. Move the energy attached to the experience; dance, run, scream into a pillow. Journal about the ways the experience affected and impacted you. Then, when you feel complete, when you feel like you've explored and allowed all there is to explore, you can finally let go.

Reflection
We let go so that we can let in. So that we can clear and make space for the experiences and information that nurtures our heart and soul. Without spending this intentional time letting go fully, we take up space in our hearts. Space that is filled with pain, when it could be filled with love and peace.

True Colours
What do you need to let go of? Take time and sit with it, explore it fully, and release it. Enjoy the opportunities found in the space you create for love and peace.

Let Your Light Shine

Intention
You are held and supported by energies bigger than you, bigger than any of us, yet we are still intricately woven within this massive universe. You are a light in this world, a world that needs your light so desperately. Take up space and let yourself shine!

Reflection
Your light has made a difference, perhaps in ways you're not even aware of. Trust that when you let your light shine, it spreads and multiplies. Thank you for that.

True Colours
Where did you shine your light, your True Colours, today?

Healing Reflection 5: Breathe Easy; You Deserve It

Bring your attention to your beautiful heart. I want you to be grateful for the love you have given and all the love you have received.

Picture a warm and loving light spreading gently from the top of your head all the way down to your toes. You are so protected. You are safe, you are held.

Picture a person you are grateful for, standing in front of you. Tell them how grateful you are for them. Let the gratitude wash over you.

The healing journey is about coming home to yourself, your true self, and remembering your wholeness. You came into the world whole and pure, and things happened to you in this life. Things that changed you, changed how you view yourself, changed how you view the world, relationships, and your sense of worth.

People did things, said things, let you down, betrayed you, people left. At times, you left yourself. You have had to protect your heart. You have worried for so long, carried so much. You have forgiven people who might not have deserved it, in order to heal yourself, but you forgot to forgive yourself. To remember it is not your fault.

It is time to put down the weight of the pain. It is time to know love without pain, without fear and suffering, without losing yourself. You put up walls when it was the only way to get to the next day. The only way to cope with the deep pain in your heart. Days when you would wake and could barely put your feet on the floor because the pain was so bad, so raw. Days where you'd lie so you wouldn't have to face it all, so you wouldn't have to put the "everything is fine" mask on. A mask that is so hard to put on, because you are so damn tired!

Picture that little you; see your little face and wrap your arms around that child who was just trying their best. Trying not to disappoint anyone. Trying to fit in. Desperate to be loved and seen and protected by someone who would cradle you in this world and make you feel safe to be yourself. Instead of feeling so lost, so much pressure, as if you were somehow falling behind. The truth is, you have always been right on time and right on track.

You have felt loss, unbearable loss. Loss that had you questioning what life is really about. Those you lost are here. They want you to heal and let go and to know that letting go does not mean loving them less. You loved so hard. You are healing in this exact moment.

You are here, loving yourself so much right now, because you deserve it. You deserve to love yourself. You are worthy of your love. People count on you to love yourself first. You are a good person, you are worthy of healing, of happiness. Healing isn't for other people; it's for you, for me, for all of humanity.

Let yourself feel it all and know that when it is moved through you, you are *free*. Free to feel lighter, free to find joy in things you didn't notice before or things you felt guilty about enjoying. Free to let smiles from within that you've been protecting for so long come out and wash across your beautiful face. To let yourself burst with gratitude. To remember that you have enough, you are enough, and you are safe and held.

Say these words out loud as a claiming of your truth:

I deserve to heal.

I am worthy of healing.

I am safe.

I am loved.

I am love.

Adversity The Teacher

Intention

Can you accept your adversarial experiences as your teachers? One of the greatest freedoms we have is to extract lessons from our journey. Seek them with intention so that your soul can check the lesson off as complete. If we miss the lessons being offered, being asked of us to learn, the experiences might reoccur, perhaps even more disruptive than the ones before.

Take pauses throughout your journey in this life. Reflect after challenges are overcome, then look for and apply the lessons. We are often so relieved when the hard stuff is over, but this part of lesson collection is critical to more peaceful waters ahead.

Reflection

You and your experiences are your greatest teacher. Love yourself hard enough to spend time to find calm in the chaos of challenge and to absorb the lessons supporting your growth and evolution.

True Colours

Look back at your challenges and more difficult experiences and look for any lessons you may have missed. Perhaps even an opportunity to know yourself in a deeper, more reflective way. Send gratitude to your heart and do something that brings you joy. Your work is paying off.

Disappointment and Worth

Intention

It is with our minds that we create our world. We don't always respond to what happens; we respond to our perception of what happens. If someone lets you down, most of us make that mean something about our worth. Our perception is that we are not good enough, loveable enough, worthy enough. This is our perception, and it is rooted in old experiences.

Of all the possible reasons why we were let down, we choose the one that denies us love. Not in a multiple choice way but as an automatic response. An automation again, rooted and programmed in old experiences. When what is likely true is that the person let you down because they're under stress, or they're preoccupied or busy.

This knowing is a beautiful opportunity to empower yourself to notice when an "I'm not worthy" response surfaces, and catch it right away! Love yourself and send a message to your heart that validates your worth and your loveable-ness!

Reflection

Dare to live more joyfully. Dare to love yourself harder and to let disappointment move through you without stories about your worth. You *are* loveable. Deal with it.

True Colours

Write "I am loveable" one thousand times. Kidding. Kind of. Whatever it takes for the message to land in your heart once and for all. I love you.

Write freely about what came up for you as you read this intention and reflection.

Enlightenment

Intention
The word "enlightenment" suggests the idea of something super-natural. However, enlightenment is simply your natural state. That's why stillness is so important to build into your daily life—through stillness, you deepen your internal state of connectedness, finding your truest nature, void of ego noise and external chaos.

The greatest obstacle to experiencing this reality is identifying with *only* your thoughts. When we identify only with our thoughts, we feed them and their energy, and we begin to think relentlessly. The key is not to ignore your mind but to practice quieting it and balancing it with the voice of your heart, your soul. You are not your mind; you are so much more. You are not your thoughts; you are not your experiences. You are light.

Reflection
Rise above thought. Thinking is just a small part of who we are. You are the peace you create every time you become still. You are the true colours you let shine in the world around you.

True Colours
What is your relationship with your mind? Does it chatter without pause? How can you access the other parts of your being, of your expansiveness?

Walk Mindfully

Intention
Walking mindfully is a way to use mindfulness in daily life. Bring awareness to how your feet connect to and move across the ground, how your breath aligns to your movement.

Invite a sense of mindfulness, presence, even meditation, to simple daily routines. The next time you wash your hands, feel the water running over them, smell the soap, feel your hands and the lather building and moving around them. Feel your fingers, the pads on your fingertips, your nails, your knuckles and palms. Give gratitude to these moments and what they connect you more deeply to.

Reflection
The power of mindfulness isn't just meant for your yoga mat or your stillness and meditation practice. It is intended to support you in realizing and witnessing every moment of now. Every step, every breath, every sweet moment of this life that has been gifted to you. Let mindfulness be your greatest tool to savour the sweetness of life.

True Colours
Where can you invite a daily practice of mindfulness? When you do one thing and that one thing only. Not letting the mind take you anywhere else than here and now. Do this and then notice how it feels.

You Are Your Future Self

Intention

You are a visionary for a bigger brighter future, a bigger, brighter tomorrow, every single day. Defining yourself by your future self. How do we do this? First look after your energy now. Are you in integrity with your values, are you aligned to your morals? Step into the energy of your future self and live it in this moment and the next. The past consumes precious real estate that your future will be built upon. Make space.

Reflection

The more you live in the energy of your future self, of who you *want* your future self to be and experience, the more you'll attract those experiences into reality. Be lovingly disciplined with your thoughts and emotions. It's an attainable path; you know the way.

True Colours

What energy do you need to shift so that it aligns with the future version of you?

Agitated Breath, Agitated Mind

Intention

Has breathing with consciousness and intention become part of your daily life? Do you notice that when you feel worried or bothered, that your breath changes? It is a response that validates the situation and confirms to your mind that things are not okay. Sometimes, things really aren't okay, and breath response is natural. Look at the moments when breath is agitated and does not need to be; when you are driving or waiting in line. Your breath is telling your mind something is very wrong, when it simply isn't. Become aware of your breath and use it as a tool to anchor you into peace.

Reflection

Breath, the tool you were born with. The tool that has been working for you all day, every day, without you even having to ask. Strengthen this connection, your use of this powerful and natural tool. In return, it will calm your nervous system, bring you peace and better sleep. It will fuel your energy and let you be right here, exactly where you are.

True Colours

Now that you are noticing your breath more often, more consciously, what is shifting? How are you using this lifelong tool in a more intentional way?

Your True Colours

Intention
Giving yourself a pat on the back now and then wouldn't hurt. Think of the grass on a lawn: you never actually see it growing, but you see its growth. We also aren't the versions of ourselves that we once were. This is an ongoing process; you *are* growing and changing, because you are choosing it. The version of you that experienced challenge, adversity, and wounding is healing in this very moment. It might not always feel like it, but like the growing grass, it's happening.

This version of you that didn't have boundaries has some boundaries now. This version of you that didn't think you were worthy or good enough is delivering a different, kinder message to your heart. You are working on *your* journey to brightening and celebrating *your* True Colours, and your growth shows. You feel it.

Let today be filled with loving pats on your back.

Reflection
You are growing and changing and evolving. You have tools now that a different version of you did not have. You did that! You continue to show up for yourself and it's making a difference.

True Colours
Write a celebration of your growth, your toolbox, your expansiveness, your healing, your light, your love . . . Your True Colours.